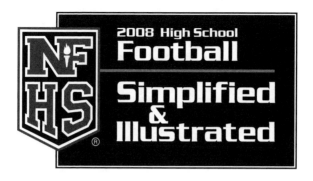

2008 High School
Football

Simplified
&
Illustrated

ROBERT F. KANABY, Publisher
Bob Colgate, Editor
NFHS Publications

To maintain the sound traditions of this sport, encourage sportsmanship and minimize the inherent risk of injury, the National Federation of State High School Associations (NFHS) writes playing rules for varsity competition among student-athletes of high school age. High school coaches, officials and administrators who have knowledge and experience regarding this particular sport and age group volunteer their time to serve on the rules committee. Member associations of the NFHS independently make decisions regarding compliance with or modification of these playing rules for the student-athletes in their respective states.

NFHS rules are used by education-based and non-education-based organizations serving children of varying skill levels who are of high school age and younger. In order to make NFHS rules skill-level and age-level appropriate, the rules may be modified by any organization that chooses to use them. Except as may be specifically noted in this rules book, the NFHS makes no recommendation about the nature or extent of the modifications that may be appropriate for children who are younger or less skilled than high school varsity athletes.

Every individual using these rules is responsible for prudent judgment with respect to each contest, athlete and facility, and each athlete is responsible for exercising caution and good sportsmanship. These rules should be interpreted and applied so as to make reasonable accommodations for disabled athletes.

2008 High School Football Rules Simplified & Illustrated

Copyright © 2008 by the National Federation of State High School Associations with the United States Copyright Office.

Major portions of this book are protected by copyrights of Referee Enterprises, Inc., and are used by permission. Copying in whole or in part is prohibited without prior written consent from Referee Enterprises, Inc. *and* the National Federation of State High School Associations. PLAYPIC™ and MECHANIGRAM™ are registered trademarks of Referee Enterprises, Inc.

Republication of all or any portion of this publication on the Internet is expressly prohibited.

Produced by Referee Enterprises Inc., publishers of *Referee* magazine.

Published by the
NATIONAL FEDERATION
OF STATE HIGH SCHOOL ASSOCIATIONS
PO Box 690
Indianapolis, IN 46206
Phone: 317-972-6900, Fax: 317.822.5700
www.nfhs.org

ISBN-13: 978-1-58208-099-4

Printed in the United States of America

Table of Contents

Each state high school association adopting these rules is the sole and exclusive source of binding rules interpretations for contests involving its member schools. Any person having questions about the interpretation of NFHS rules should contact the rules interpreter designated by his or her state high school association.

The NFHS is the sole and exclusive source of model interpretations of NFHS rules. State rules interpreters may contact the NFHS for model rules interpretations. No other model rules interpretations should be considered.

2008 NFHS Football Rules Changes

1-2-3a	White is the recommended color for all field markings. The rule continues to allow the use of other colors for field markings, when appropriate.
1-2-3d; **NEW 2-26-8**	The restraining line can now be either solid or broken. It is recommended that a broken line be used and marked by placing 12-inch-long lines separated at 24-inch intervals. Only game officials are allowed in the area marked by the restraining line.
1-5-1b,d,h	Hip pads, tailbone protector, knee pads and thigh guards must not be altered from the manufacturer's original design/production. Shinguards, if worn, must meet NOCSAE specifications.
1-5-2b, NOTE	A hand pad is now defined as a covering for the hand which may have separate openings for each finger and thumb, is absent of any web-like material between the fingers and/or thumb, and not covering each finger and thumb. The implementation date for a mandatory securely attached label or stamp has been changed from 2008 to 2012.
2-16-2e; 3-3-4b; **8-2-2; 8-2-3;** **10-2-4**	Four changes in the playing rules were refined regarding the penalty options for teams that score but were fouled during the play. Rule 2-16-2e was clarified (along with Rule 10-2-4) to revise the definition of a multiple foul to stipulate that a team must foul twice during the same down to commit multiple fouls. Rule 3-3-4b was amended to clarify issues at the end of the half, and along with amendments to Rules 8-2-2 and 8-2-3, clearly stipulate that fouls by the opponent of the scoring team on the last timed down of the first half can carry over to the second-half kickoff, however fouls by the opponent of the scoring team on the last timed down of the second half cannot carry over to overtime.
3-5-1	The option to carry over unused second-half time-outs into overtime has been removed. The NFHS-recommended Resolving Tied Games procedure continues to provide for one time-out per overtime period with the revisions stipulating that unused time-outs do not carry to subsequent overtime periods.
3-5-2a, NOTE	The head coach can now designate another coach for the purpose of requesting time-outs. The designee shall remain in place for the entire game except in case of emergency.
4-2-3	The inadvertent whistle rule has been clarified. The new wording indicates the options available in a simpler form and makes the choosing of an option an easier process to understand.

9-9 PENALTY	Hiding the ball under the jersey will now be enforced as a basic spot foul using the all-but-one principle.
New 9-9-4; 9-9 PENALTY	No player shall use a kicking tee in violation of Rule 1-3-4. The use of an illegal kicking tee will now be penalized as an unfair act committed by the player. Acceptance of this foul on a try or field goal will nullify any points scored, with the penalty enforced as a basic spot foul using the all-but-one principle.
10-4-6; 10-4-7	The change to Rule 10-4-6 allows the same enforcement for either team by defining the basic spot as the 20-yard line for this type of foul (15-yard line in nine-, eight-, and six-player). A change to Rule 10-4-7 helps clarify the basic spot on running plays for fouls by the opponent of the team in possession when the team in possession puts the ball in the end zone and, subsequently, possession is lost.

Editorial and Other Changes

1-5-1a; 1-5-1f-1b; 1-5-1f2; 1-5-3b; 1-5-3c; 1-5-3l-3; 1-5-4; 1-6-1, 2; 2-13-1; 2-16-2h5; 2-22; 2-29-1, 2, 3; NEW 2-34-3; 3-3-3a; 3-4-2; 3-5-10c; 6-1 PENALTY; 7-2-5; 7-3-2b; 7-5-13; Table 7-5 #4; 8-3-5b; 9-4 PENALTY; 9-9-1; 10-2-1, 2, 3, 4; 10-5-1g, h, i; FUNDAMENTALS X-8; 9-, 8-, and 6-player NEW Rule 10; Penalty Summary; OFFICIAL FOOTBALL SIGNALS – 10, 47

Points of Emphasis

1. MRSA and Communicable Skin Conditions
2. Purpose of a Football Helmet
3. Altering Legal Football Equipment
4. Sideline Management and Control
5. False Starts, Shifts and Motion

Part 1

New or Revised NFHS Rules

This simplified and illustrated book is a supplement to the 2008 NFHS football rules book. As such, it is intended to aid in the administration of the game and in the standardization of interpretations through a unique method of presenting rules.

Each year the NFHS Football Rules Committee considers many items which are submitted as potential changes or revisions. The items which secured favorable endorsement are listed on pages 6 and 7. The majority of illustrations in Part 1 show these changes and revisions.

The NFHS Football Rules Committee also identified areas of concern which are designated as "Points of Emphasis" for the current season. They appear in Part 2. However, no rule changes were made to cover these particular items.

The illustrations found in Part 3 of this book have been revised to reflect any changes or clarifications as directed by the NFHS Football Rules Committee. Recent interpretations have been added to keep the contents current.

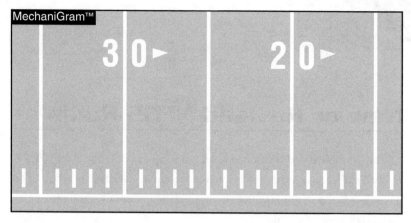

1-2-3a Lines shall be marked with a noncaustic, nontoxic material designed for marking fields such as powdered gypsum, calcium carbonate and liquid aerosol paint. It is recommended that these lines be white.

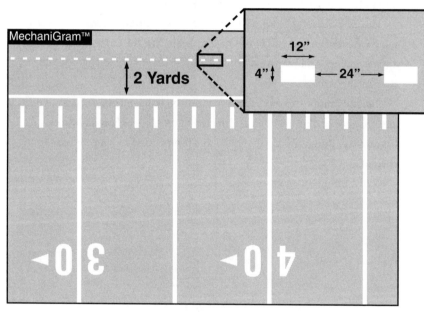

1-2-3d It is recommended that the restraining line be marked by placing 12-inch-long lines, separated at 24-inch intervals.

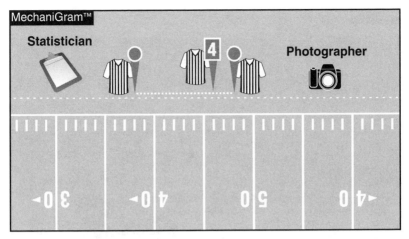

2-26-8, 9-8-3 A restraining line is a line placed around the outside of the field. No person, including but not limited to, spectators, game administrators or members of the media, shall be allowed within the restraining line. A maximum of three coaches as well as permitted nonplayers are allowed within the restraining line in front of the team box, as provided for in Rule 9-8-3.

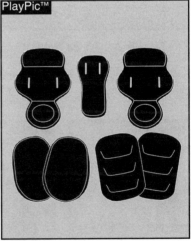

1-5-1b, 1-5-1d, 1-5-1h Hip pads and tailbone protector, knee pads, and thigh guards must be unaltered from the manufacturer's original design/production.

2-6-2a, 3-5-2a, 3-5-2a Note When the head coach is not on the sideline, the head coach may designate someone to request time-outs from the sideline. The designee shall remain in place for the entire game except in case of emergency.

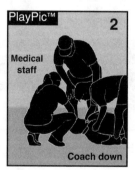

2-6-2a, 3-5-2a, 3-5-2a Note If the head coach is not on the sideline, such as due to a disqualification (1) or injury (2), the head coach may designate someone to request time-outs from the sideline (3). The designee shall remain in place for the entire game except in case of emergency.

2-16-2e, 10-2-4 It is a multiple foul when two or more live-ball fouls (other than nonplayer or unsportsmanlike) are committed during the same down by the same team (1). One penalty must be declined (2) as only one may be enforced (3).

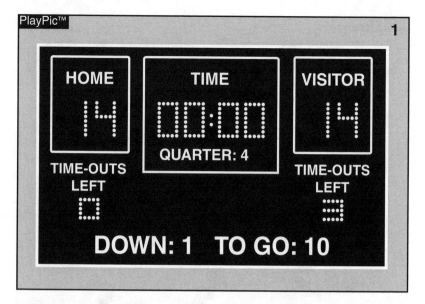

3-5-1 Each team is entitled to three charged team timeouts during each half. Unused first half time-outs cannot be used in the second half. Unused second half time-outs cannot be used in overtime. The visiting team had all three charged team time-outs remaining in the second half and the home team had none (1). Each team is entitled to one charged team time-out in the first overtime period (2).

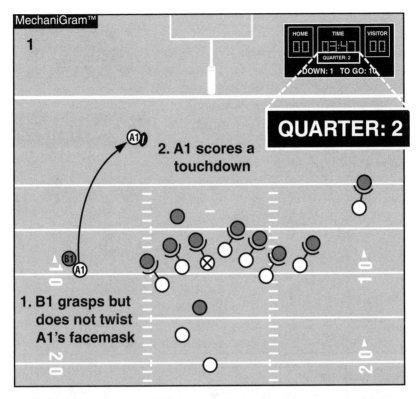

MechaniGram™ 1

2. A1 scores a touchdown

QUARTER: 2

1. B1 grasps but does not twist A1's facemask

HOME 00 · TIME 03:47 QUARTER: 2 · VISITOR 00
DOWN: 1 TO GO: 10

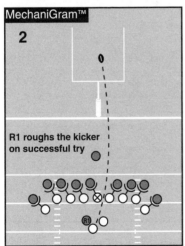

MechaniGram™ 2

R1 roughs the kicker on successful try

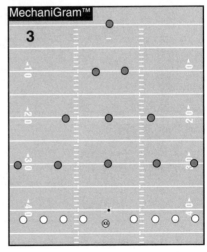

MechaniGram™ 3

2-16-2e, 8-2-2, 8-2-3, 10-2-4 The opponent of the scoring team commits a live-ball foul during a down in which there was no change of possession (1). The same team commits a live-ball foul during the try (2). Both penalties may be enforced on the subsequent kickoff (3).

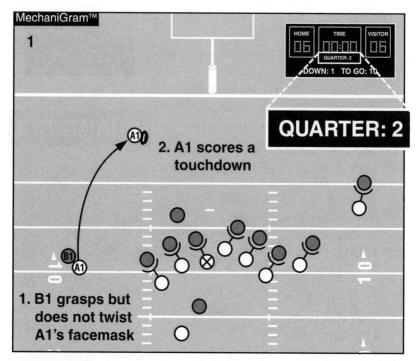

MechaniGram™

1

HOME **06**

TIME **00:00**

QUARTER: 2

VISITOR **06**

DOWN: 1 TO GO: 10

QUARTER: 2

2. A1 scores a touchdown

1. B1 grasps but does not twist A1's facemask

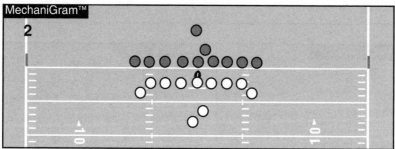

MechaniGram™

2

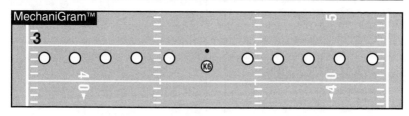

MechaniGram™

3

8-2-2 The opponent of the scoring team commits a live-ball foul during the last timed down of the second quarter and there was no change of possession (1). The penalty may be enforced on the try (2) or on the subsequent kickoff to start the second half (3).

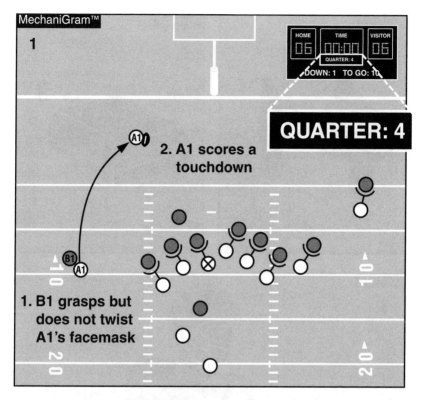

MechaniGram™

1

HOME **06** TIME **00:00** VISITOR **06**

QUARTER: 4

DOWN: 1 TO GO: 10

QUARTER: 4

2. A1 scores a touchdown

1. B1 grasps but does not twist A1's facemask

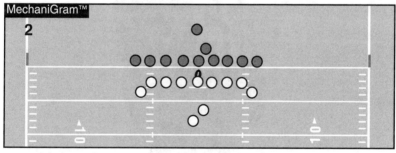

MechaniGram™

2

8-2-2 The opponent of the scoring team commits a live-ball foul during the last timed down of the fourth quarter and there was no change of possession (1). By rule, the penalty must be enforced on the try (2).

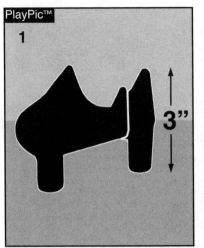

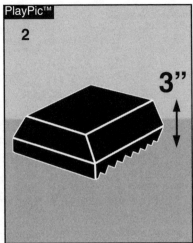

9-9-3, 9-9-4, PENALTY 9-9 Use of illegal kicking tees (1 and 2) results in a 15-yard penalty enforced under the all-but-one principle. Hiding the ball under a jersey (3) is also an unfair act. The penalty is 15 yards enforced under the all-but-one principle.

Part 2

2008 NFHS Points of Emphasis

1. MRSA and Communicable Skin Conditions

Methecillin-Resistant Staphylococcus Aurues (MRSA) is a relatively new problem in our communities and in the sports world. However, it is an increasingly more common problem with potentially serious consequences. The risk to athletes can be reduced dramatically by proper preventive measures, early identification, precautions to minimize spread to team members and opponents, and quick and appropriate treatment. The NFHS Sports Medicine Advisory Committee (SMAC) has developed multiple position and policy statements on this topic and that of communicable skin diseases in general over the past few years. These can be found on the NFHS Web site under Sports Medicine. One of the very first pages of the NFHS rules book deals with this issue.

MRSA represents the evolution of a common bacteria, "Staph" to an aggressive and resistant bacteria. This has occurred, in part, because of the widespread use of antibiotics. As the sensitive or "easy staph" is killed, the stronger more virulent ones that are resistant to penicillin and standard antibiotics grow stronger and more aggressive. Scientists continue to develop new antibiotics to attack these stubborn bacteria, but it is a race in which scientists need help to stay ahead of the resistant bacteria. Judicious use of antibiotics, as well as measures discussed in this point of emphasis, can help everyone be safer from communicable diseases of all types, especially the more dangerous ones like MRSA.

Most skin infections are transmitted by skin-to-skin contact or by contact with equipment that has the "germ" present. Skin is a very strong protective organ in the body, but the risk of transmission of bacteria, fungus and viruses is greater if the integrity of the skin is weakened by a scrape, scratch or other open place. Football, because of the equipment, and wrestling, because of the extensive skin-to-skin contact and the wrestling mat, are considered the highest risk sports for MRSA and other skin diseases like ringworm (tinea corporis), herpes simplex and herpes gladiatorum, and impetigo.

Prevention of Contracting Skin Infections

In medicine, prevention is always considered the best treatment for any disorder, when possible. Basic hygienic principles are the foundation to help reduce/prevent the development and spread of these infectious diseases. Individual athletes need to shower after each event or practice, use their own soap or use a liquid soap from a dispenser and not community bar soap to shower, avoid sharing towels and other items, have all open wounds or abrasions evaluated by the coach or certified athletic trainer before each practice or competition, and use clean undergarments with each practice or contest.

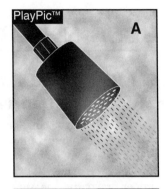

Prevention of Spread of Skin Infections

The only thing worse for a coach and a team than having one player out of action because of a skin infection is to have multiple players coming down with infections that lead to loss of playing time and/or serious health issues for the individuals and the team. Therefore, early identification of the illness, quick removal from exposure of teammates, proper cleaning of individual equipment and shared equipment as well as appropriate treatment of the infected individuals is critical. It is impossible to know exactly when a lesion is no longer contagious to others, but minimal treatment regimens have been suggested before allowing athletes to return to play. (See next page)

Two ways of preventing skin infections: showering using soap from a dispenser or a non-shared bar (A) and laundering undergarments so that clean attire is worn for each practice or contest (B).

Universal precautions should be used by all concerned to minimize the likelihood of skin infection spreading.

Treatment

The appropriate use of antibiotics is the mainstay for treating MRSA and other bacterial infections of the skin. Topical and/or oral anti-fungal medications can be helpful in treating ringworm. In certain situations, anti-viral medications may be used for such viral infections as herpes gladiatorum and herpes simplex. Even then, wounds and lesions should be covered to protect all involved. If lesions do not respond as suggested by the physician, a return visit for further evaluation should be considered as this might suggest resistant infections such as MRSA.

Hygienic Principles That Should Be Followed By All Coaches and Athletes

Following these guidelines will help reduce the occurrences and outbreaks of infectious diseases. This will take active participation of the coach, parent and athlete. Together this will create a healthy environment that will allow the athlete to compete and reduce the risk of being sidelined.

Individual Athletes

• Any lesion, scrape or wound on the skin should be evaluated by a certified athletic trainer or physician.

• Seek medical care as soon as possible for personal safety and to protect teammates.

• Don't return to action until advised to do so by a physician.

• If lesion is not clearing as expected, return for additional medical consultation as failure to respond can be a sign of MRSA.

• Coach should be made aware of any lesion considered infectious.

• Shower after every practice or contest, as soon as possible.

• Use clean gear and undergarments for every practice or contest.

• Avoid cosmetic shaving (genital area, chest, legs).

• Use soap from a container, not bar soap.

• Don't share toiletries, towels or other equipment.

• Don't use a whirlpool or cold tub with any open wounds, scrapes or scratches.

• Shower before using whirlpools or common tubs.

• All abrasions or cuts must be properly cleansed and covered before practice/competition.

Coaches, Certified Athletic Trainers, and Other Personnel

• Monitor athletes for possible infected lesions through reporting by the athlete or medical personnel.

• Withdraw any athlete with a suspicious skin lesion until evaluated by a physician.

• Clean mats, and equipment on a regular basis with appropriate disinfectants (1:100 solution of bleach like Clorox made up fresh daily).

• If an infection has occurred in a team member, check other athletes daily before practice.

• If several athletes develop infection with the same organism, seek consultation with physician or health department as soon as possible to eradicate spread. They may suggest special techniques to eradicate the bacteria from the skin and/or nose of team members or other epidemiological studies with cultures, etc.

• Make sure athletes are cleared by physician before returning them to practice or games. This protects everyone, including team members.

• Even after medical clearance, keep lesions covered until skin is covered over and wound is healed.

• Always use "universal precautions" when dealing with a skin lesion as one would with blood and other bodily fluids. This means gloves, hand washing, proper disposal of contaminated equipment in plastic and/or bio-hazard bags.

• If lesions are detected in your team, notify appropriate personnel at opposing school(s) within a 2-3 day period of a previous contest with that school(s).

2. Purpose of a Football Helmet

In almost all articles and publications regarding the proper use and fit of the football helmet, the focus has been on the coach and his/her obligation to inform players of the risks of serious and sometimes

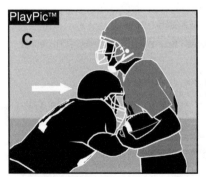
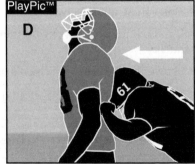

Face tackling (C) and spearing (D) are dangerous acts that must not be condoned or practiced. Football helmets are not intended to be used as weapons.

catastrophic injury when a player leads with the head during contact. The rules against a player butting, ramming or spearing an opponent with the football helmet are there to protect that player, as well as the opponent. A ball carrier using the helmet as a weapon to punish a tackler is seldom penalized but should be addressed just as most officials address the act of a tackler using the football helmet as a weapon to punish a ball carrier. It is critical that officials penalize a player that uses the helmet as a weapon, whether a player is in the capacity of either a tackler or a ball carrier. Coaches and officials must collaborate to protect the player by teaching proper techniques and penalizing improper use of the football helmet.

3. Altering Legal Football Equipment

Greater emphasis must be placed on the role coaches, officials and players have in not only wearing mandatory equipment as specified in the NFHS Football Rules Book, but in wearing it properly. Safety is everyone's responsibility. Football equipment, such as knee pads, thigh pads and hip pads with tailbone protector should be worn as manufactured and may not be modified. Similarly, coaches, officials and players must be aware of illegal equipment or adornments, as specified in the rules.

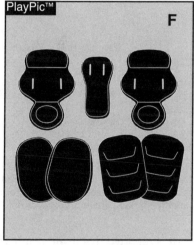

Required equipment must be not be altered from the manufacturer's original design/production (E). Knee pads, thigh pads, hip pads with tailbone protector and other equipment (F) should be worn as manufactured and may not be modified.

Officials should observe players during the game in an attempt to verify mandatory equipment is being properly worn. Prior to any snap or free kick, players having illegal or improperly worn equipment shall be required to immediately rectify the problem or leave the game and not return until they are compliant. Officials who cannot verify compliance by participating players prior to the snap or free kick, must call a foul and penalize it, accordingly, if they see a violation during a down.

4. Sideline Management and Control

The NFHS Football Rules Committee feels that a review of the team box, the coaches' box, sideline control and management issues is necessary. Reports from the nation's playing fields suggest that sideline control needs continued improvement. Not only are coaches and others violating the rules, but officials are not consistently enforcing the rules! Congestion by non-players on the sidelines is also a problem as the media, boosters and others crowd, not only the sideline, but onto the playing field as well.

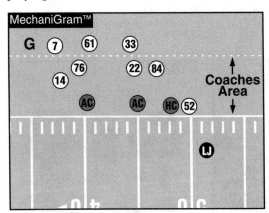

Nonplayers such as numbers 14, 76, 22 and 84 may not be in the coaches area. Number 52 may be in the coaches area if he is about to become a player or is returning as a replaced player (G). For any violation, the official should drop his penalty marker (H) and the appropriate warning or penalty should be enforced.

It is reported that team members and coaches are encroaching on the playing field during play resulting in more collisions between coaches and officials as well as team members obstructing officials' space on the sideline. Certainly, this is a safety concern for ALL! A number of coaches have had collisions resulting in serious injuries because non-players were so close the coaches couldn't get away from the play. It also is a logistical problem for officials who must have free access to the sidelines to effectively officiate their areas.

Rule 1-2 clearly offers complete parameters of the playing field, outside the field of play and surrounding area. Rule 9-8-3 emphatically specifies that only three coaches are allowed in the coaches' box, which is the two-yard belt between the 25-yard lines.

Consequences and penalties for team box and sideline violations are prescribed in the penalty section of Rule 9-8. There is a progressive component to the penalties for these violations, but they must be consistently enforced to be effective. It seems that all too often, officials look the other way and disregard these violations and that simply makes the problem worse. Officials need to communicate their expectations with the coaches before the game and early in the contest, but when said expectations are not met, they must be penalized.

Another related problem is the growing number of media, photographers, statisticians and school boosters populating the sidelines. This is a game management problem that game administrators should address, but game officials must alert game management immediately when the situation is noticed. Game administrators and school officials are reminded that the 4-inch-wide restraining line around the outside of the playing area is MANDATORY and that no one other than officials is to be inside the line. Properly marking this line will help everyone involved more easily manage the area around the field.

Coaches and players must recognize and be aware of team and coaching box rules that are in effect during the contest. The burden is on the head coach to remind coaches and players of these rules. Authorized conferences must be conducted properly and within the limits of the rule. Officials must be more vigilant and enforce the rules applicable to sideline management. Game management must do its part to clearly mark and maintain the field throughout the season. These efforts will minimize risk, lead to more effective officiating, and can prevent unfortunate incidents, which may result in serious injury.

5. False Starts, Shifts and Motion

Offensive football alignments have become so diversified that more emphasis has to be placed upon legally starting a free kick down and a scrimmage down. There is not much that officials can do once a down is in progress except to call and penalize fouls that occur.

It should be a point of emphasis for all officials to make sure that a team starts a down legally. The areas that need to be given special attention are encroachment, illegal shifts, false starts and illegal motion.

Encroachment

Encroachment is a foul for being illegally in the neutral zone. The neutral zone, free kick lines and scrimmage lines are all established when the ball is marked ready for play. The neutral zone is that 10-yard space between the two free-kick lines during a free-kick down, and the length of a football space between the two scrimmage lines during a scrimmage down.

The neutral zone is established and encroachment restrictions are in effect when the ready-for-play signal has been sounded. Once the ready-for-play signal has been sounded, no player shall encroach on the neutral zone by touching the ball, an opponent, or by being in the neutral zone to give defensive signals.

The neutral zone, that space the length of a football, is established once the ready-for-play signal has been sounded, but the planes of the neutral zone lines are not established until the snapper has placed his or her hand(s) on the ball. Following the ready-for-play signal and after the snapper has placed his or her hand(s) on the ball, no player may break the plane of the neutral zone lines other than the snapper. During a scrimmage down, the snapper is the only player who may have any part of his or her person in the neutral zone. The snapper's hand(s) on the ball may be beyond the foremost point of the ball.

After the ball is ready for play for a scrimmage down, but prior to the snapper placing his or her hand(s) on the ball, it is encroachment if a defender enters the neutral zone to give defensive signals or places his or her hand(s) on the ground so that contact is made with the ball or an opponent.

After the ball is ready for play for a scrimmage down, but prior to the snapper placing his or her hand(s) on the ball, it is not encroachment if either an offensive player or a defender breaks the plane of the neutral zone. Both players may adjust their positions and get back behind the neutral zone except for the defender as mentioned above, because the planes of the neutral zone lines are not established until after the ready-for-play signal has sounded and the snapper has placed his or her hand(s) on the ball.

Either an offensive player or a defender, who was on the opponent's side of the neutral zone conferring with his or her coach at the sideline, may cross through the neutral zone to his or her team's huddle without encroaching prior to the snapper placing his or her hand(s) on the ball after the ready-for-play signal. But once the snapper has placed his or her hand(s) on the ball following the ready-for-play signal for a scrimmage down, it is a foul for encroachment if any player breaks the plane of the neutral zone or any player, who was conferring with his or her coach at the sideline on the opponent's side of the neutral zone passes through the neutral zone to his or her huddle.

During a free-kick down after the ball has been marked ready for play, it is permissible for the place-kick holder or the kicker to be beyond his or her free-kick line prior to the time the ball is kicked. It is encroachment for any other player to be beyond his or her free-kick line prior to the ball being kicked.

It is not encroachment for a substitute or a replaced player to cross through the neutral zone. A substitute cannot encroach until after he or she is established as a player on his or her team's side of the neutral zone. Encroachment is a dead-ball foul resulting in a 5-yard penalty from the succeeding spot.

Shifts

A shift is a maneuver employed by the offensive team to take new set positions, and some type of shift is employed by the offense on almost every down. The offensive players who are most frequently involved in a shift are the backfield players and the players on the ends of the line of scrimmage. But what about interior linemen, those players on the line positioned between the snapper and the player on the end of the line who have placed a hand(s) on or near the ground. Can they legally be involved in a shift?

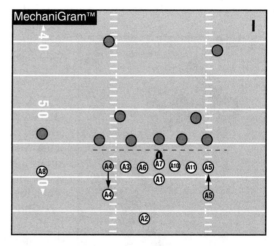

After a shift (I), all 11 players of A must come to an absolute stop and remain stationary simultaneously without movement of hands, feet, head or body for at least one second before the snap.

Let's take a thorough look at the shift Rule 2-39 and that aspect of the false start Rule 7-1-7c which has complicated the enforcement of the shift rule. This shouldn't be the case because these are two separate rules.

The shift Rule of 2-39 plainly states that a shift is the action of one or more offensive players, who after a huddle or after taking set positions, move to a new set position before the ensuing snap. Nowhere do the rules define a set position, so the necessary inference is that a set position may be either a two-, three-, or a four-point stance. The shift rule says that after a huddle or after assuming a set position, which may be either a two-, three-, or a four-point stance, one or more offensive players may move to a new set position(s) and remain absolutely stationary for at least one second prior to the snap.

Another aspect of enforcing the shift rule is Rule 7-1-7c. This rule deals with a false start. It says that any offensive player on the line of scrimmage between the snapper and the player on the end of the line who, after placing a hand(s) on or near the ground, moves or lifts the hand(s) or makes any quick movement, commits a false start.

Rule 7-1-7c does not prevent a shift. It is referring to that final set position assumed either without a shift or following a shift(s) that occurred. After assuming this final set position whether a shift(s) have occurred or not, a false start occurs if any player on the offensive line between the snapper and the player on the end of the line were to move or lift a hand(s) after placing the hand(s) on or near the ground.

There is no limit on the number of shifts that the offensive team may execute prior to the snap. The only factor that makes a shift illegal is the element of time. All shifts must be concluded and all 11 offensive players must be stationary for at least one full second prior to the snap. The only shift that can be illegal is the one just prior to the snap.

A shift occurs whenever the offensive team breaks the huddle and assumes a pre-snap position; when linemen or backs move from an upright position to a position with hands on knees or thighs; when linemen or backs move from a position with hands on knees or thighs to a three- or four-point down position; when a player who is positioned on the end of the line moves along the line or to a position in the backfield; when a backfield player moves from one position in the backfield to another or moves from a position in the backfield to a position on the line; and when the quarterback moves from an upright position to a

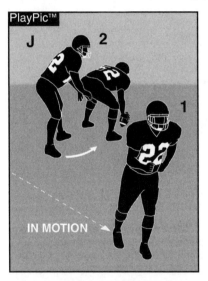

The shift depicted in (J) is illegal. When the back (1) goes in motion and the quarterback then steps up under the center (2), it is a foul because the back had not been set for at least one second.

position with hands under the snapper. If the quarterback were to shift in this manner while another player is moving, a foul for illegal motion occurs if the ball were to be snapped before both players had stopped and were motionless for at least one second prior to the snap.

All shifts must be done in a manner that does not simulate action at the snap. Remember, no shift is illegal unless all offensive players fail to be simultaneously stationary as required for at least one full second prior to the snap. The manner in which players shift can be false starts, but it cannot be an illegal shift.

Following a shift, if a player were to go in motion before all 11 players are set for at least one second, an illegal shift occurs if this player is still moving at the snap. Anytime there is more than one player moving before the snap, all 11 players must be motionless simultaneously for at least one second prior to the snap.

An illegal shift is always a live-ball foul occurring at the snap, resulting in a 5-yard penalty from the previous spot.

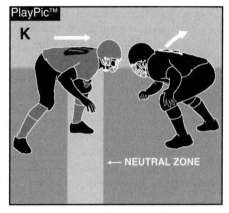

In (K), encroachment by the defensive player (left) causes the offensive player to false start. In that case, only the encroachment is penalized.

False Starts

Rule 7-1-7 is clear as to what constitutes a false start. A false start occurs if a player commits a shift or feigned charge simulating action at the snap, if any player's act is clearly intended to cause the defender(s) to encroach, or when any offensive player(s) on the line between the snapper and the player on the end of the line, after placing his or her hand(s) on or near the ground, moves his or her hand(s) or makes any quick movement. This last statement is referring to that final set position prior to the snap that is assumed without a previous shift occurring or after a previous shift has occurred.

The major problem in dealing with false starts is the inconsistency in administration. Whether or not a false start has occurred is not predicated upon whether the defender encroaches or not, or by the down and/or distance. The false start act has to be judged on its own. The offensive team is obligated to move, shift, or go in motion in such a manner that does not simulate action at the snap. Whenever the false start causes a defender to encroach, only the false start is penalized.

After the ready-for-play signal has sounded and all offensive players have assumed their final set position for the snap, no player shall make a quick and/or jerky movement before the snap. The purpose for restricting such movement is to discourage action designed to cause defenders to encroach.

If the offensive team executes a shift in such a manner that simulates action at the snap, the foul is a false start and not an illegal shift. The manner in which offensive players execute shifts or go in motion can be fouls for a false start, but never for illegal shifts.

When linemen or backs initially set in an upright position or hands-on-knees position and then drop into a three- or four-point stance for their final position, the action results in a false start if it is done in a manner that simulates action at the snap. Such action must be slow and deliberate.

When the quarterback drops from an upright position to a position under the snapper, his or her action must not simulate action at the snap or a false start has occurred. When the quarterback withdraws his or her hands from underneath the snapper to go in motion, their action must be deliberate and done in a manner not simulating the start of a down, and is considered a shift. When the quarterback, while having his or her hands underneath the snapper uses jerky movements of their head, arms or body while verbally sounding his signals commits a foul. This action simulating a snap is a foul for a false start. Once the interior linemen have assumed their final pre-snap set position on the line between the snapper and the player on the end of the line and having placed their hand(s) on or near the ground, they are locked into that position and may not move their hand(s) or make any quick movement without committing a false start.

Remember the snapper is not restricted as are the interior linemen in regard to the lifting of a hand(s) placed on or near the ground. A false start is always a dead-ball foul occurring before the snap and resulting in a 5-yard penalty from the succeeding spot.

Motion

Legal motion at the snap is allowed by rule as an offensive maneuver. Only one offensive player – either a back or a player on the end of the line, but no interior linemen – may be in motion at the snap, and then, only if such motion is not toward his opponent's goal line.

Except for the quarterback under the snapper, the player in motion who started from a position not clearly behind the line of scrimmage and did not establish himself as a back by stopping for at least one full second, must be at least 5 yards behind the line of scrimmage at the snap. Either a player legally in the backfield or a player legally on the end of the line of scrimmage may go in motion if these previous requirements are satisfied.

Illegal motion occurs whenever the quarterback steps forward placing his or her hands under the snapper at the instant the snap is made. If the quarterback places his or her hands under the snapper without stepping forward, it will be a shift and not motion. If the quarterback steps forward and places their hands under the snapper and the snap is made after they are motionless for one second, the action is legal. If the quarterback with his hands under the snapper were to step backward with one foot as the snap is made, this action would be legal provided no teammate is also moving at the snap. Illegal motion occurs when any player in motion is moving toward the opponent's goal line at the snap. It is also illegal motion if an end goes in motion and is not at least 5-yards behind the line at the snap unless he or she stops and positions himself or herself as a back for at least one full second prior to the snap.

A player's motion movement can be such that his or her head and body are facing the sideline to which he or she is moving, or a sliding movement while he or she is facing the opponent's goal line, or the direction of his or her motion may change several times before the snap. Illegal motion is always a live-ball foul occurring at the snap resulting in a 5-yard penalty from the previous spot.

Part 3
Rule 1

The Game, Field, Players and Equipment

The origin of the game of football is not clear. Football, as played in the United States, is a blend of soccer and rugby, with other variations making it a truly unique sport. Football is played with an inflated ball by two teams of 11 players each on a rectangular field 360 by 160 feet. The specific lines and marks are found on the Official NFHS Field Diagram.

Player equipment has a double purpose. It must protect the wearer and also other players against the dangers of unnecessary injury. The rules are constantly reviewed and often revised to allow use of new equipment which has been developed to provide greater protection to the participants. It is the responsibility of the rules committee to specify equipment to protect players whether on offense or defense. Because past rules committees have met this responsibility, there has been a continuous improvement in football player equipment.

The game is administered by officials whose duties are outlined in the rules book and officials manual. Game officials must accept the responsibility of enforcing the letter, as well as the spirit, of the rules promptly and consistently. The safety of players is paramount and with this there can be no compromise. A thorough study and understanding of all the NFHS football publications is necessary to meet this responsibility.

1-1-7,8 The game officials shall assume authority for the contest, including penalizing unsportsmanlike acts, 30 minutes prior to the scheduled game time or as soon thereafter as they are able to be present. This jurisdiction extends through the referee's declaration of the end of the fourth period or overtime.

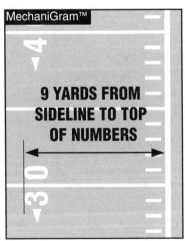

9 YARDS FROM SIDELINE TO TOP OF NUMBERS

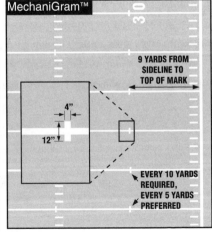

9 YARDS FROM SIDELINE TO TOP OF MARK

4"

12"

EVERY 10 YARDS REQUIRED, EVERY 5 YARDS PREFERRED

1-2-3f Nine-yard marks or numbers are required for all fields.

1-2-3h Advertising or commercial markings in the end zones (1) are allowed as they are on the field but not in the field of play and shall be no closer than 2 feet to the boundary and the goal lines. Advertising or commercial markings, such as that in (2), are prohibited on the field of play (from goalline to goalline and between the boundary lines).

1-3-2 It is permissible for either team to have an additional ball(s) approved during the course of the game. When weather conditions change it is often necessary to use a different ball. In normal situations the referee will approve and mark the balls before game time.

1-3-7 State associations may authorize use of supplementary equipment to aid in game administration. The microphone on the referee and the 25-second field clock are just two examples of equipment which can be used when properly authorized.

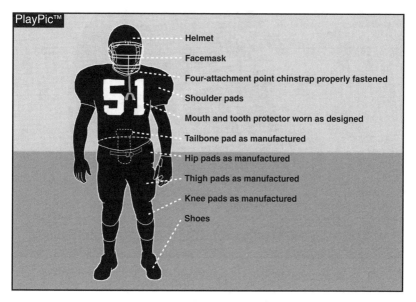

1-5-1 The items of equipment shown must be worn by all players. Four-attachment point chin straps are required and all four attachment points must be fastened. A player may not participate unless he is wearing all required equipment which is professionally manufactured and not altered to decrease protection.

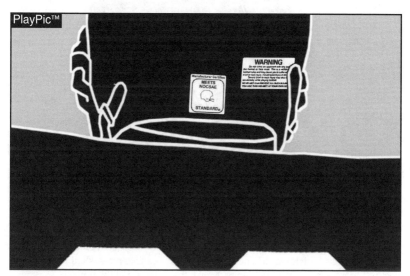

1-5-1a Note A visible, exterior warning label is required on each player's helmet. The warning label is a statement concerning the risk of injury. The coach's pregame verification to the referee and umpire that all players are equipped in compliance with the rules includes the exterior warning label.

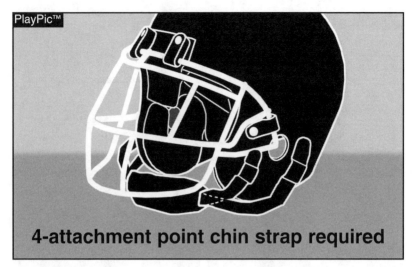

4-attachment point chin strap required

1-5-1a At least a four-attachment point chin strap shall be required to secure the helmet.

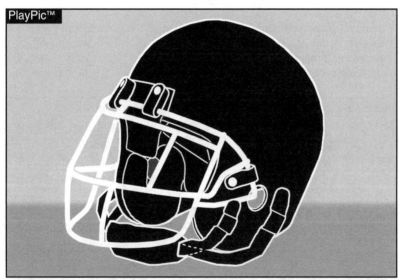

1-5-1a, Note A face mask which met the NOCSAE* test standard at the time of manufacture is required. The face mask shall be made of material designed to be nonbreakable with rounded edges, and those constructed of metal shall have the surface covered with resilient material designed to prevent chipping, burrs or abrasiveness which would endanger players. The face mask shall be properly secured to a helmet which met the NOCSAE test standard at the time of manufacture and has a visible exterior warning label regarding the risk of injury. The helmet shall be secured by a properly fastened chin strap with at least four attachment points.

*National Operating Committee on Standards for Athletic Equipment

1-5-1c These jersey numerals are legal. Different styles of numerals also are legal as long as they are Arabic numbers 1 through 99 and they are clearly visible and legible. All players of one team must wear numbers identical in style front and back and no teammates may partcipate wearing identical numbers.

1-5-1c1 The number on each jersey shall be clearly visible and legible. The jersey on the left is illegal because the number shall also be centered on the jersey horizontally, as in the jersey on the right.

1-5-1i A tooth and mouth protector (intraoral) which shall include an occlusal (protecting and separating the biting surfaces) and a labial (protecting the teeth and supporting structures) portion and covers the posterior teeth with adequate thickness is required. It is recommended the protector be properly fitted and constructed from a model made from an impression of the individual's teeth and constructed and fitted to the individual by impressing the teeth into the tooth and mouth protector itself.

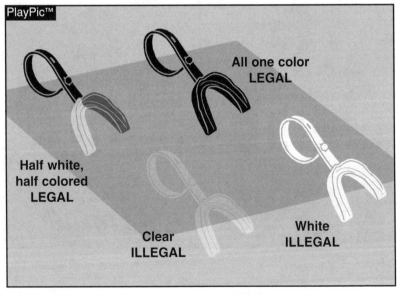

1-5-1i Tooth and mouth protectors shall be of any readily visible color, other than completely white or completely clear.

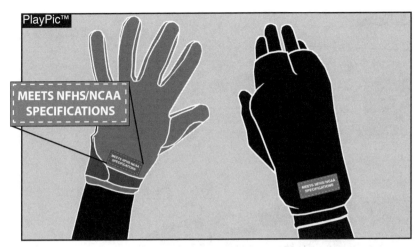

MEETS NFHS/NCAA
SPECIFICATIONS

1-5-2a,b Gloves (left) must have a securely attached label/stamp on inside or outside showing compliance with Sporting Goods Manufacturers Association (SGMA) test specifications. Gloves made of unaltered plain cloth do not need the label. Starting in 2012, hand pads (right) must carry the same label/stamp unless made of unaltered plain cloth.

1-5-3b Note 2 With state association authorization and in conjunction with a licensed medical physician, a device may be attached to a player's helmet to enhance the efficiency of a required hearing aid. The device may not provide for direct communication to or from anyone else; its function is simply to allow the hearing-impaired player to hear more efficiently.

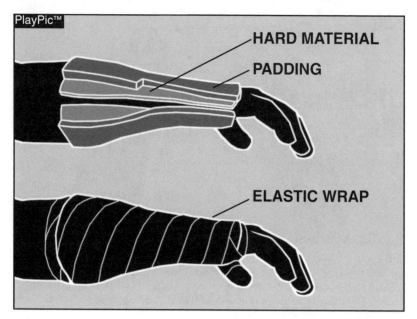

HARD MATERIAL
PADDING
ELASTIC WRAP

1-5-3c Hard material may be used on a hand, wrist, forearm or elbow cast/splint if covered on all exterior surfaces with no less than 1/2-inch thick, high-density, closed-cell polyurethane or alternate material with similar properties. Authorization from a licensed medical physician must be presented to the umpire before the game.

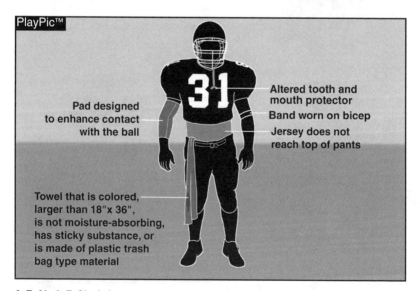

Pad designed to enhance contact with the ball

Altered tooth and mouth protector

Band worn on bicep

Jersey does not reach top of pants

Towel that is colored, larger than 18"x 36", is not moisture-absorbing, has sticky substance, or is made of plastic trash bag type material

1-5-1i; 1-5-3h, i, k No player may participate while wearing illegal equipment, an illegal uniform or with equipment that has been illegally altered.

 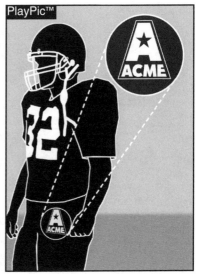

1-5-3l Jerseys/pants may have only one reference to the manufacturer and the reference on each may not exceed 2-1/4 square inches. The references shown are too large and would be illegal.

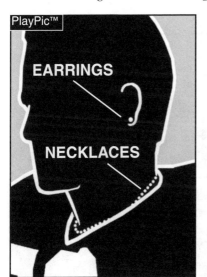

EARRINGS

NECKLACES

RINGS

BRACELETS —

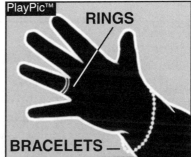

MEDICAL ALERT

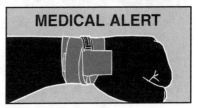

1-5-3m Jewelry such as earrings, necklaces, bracelets and rings shall not be worn. Religious and medical-alert medals are not considered jewelry. A religious medal must be taped and worn under the uniform. A medical-alert medal must be taped and may be visible.

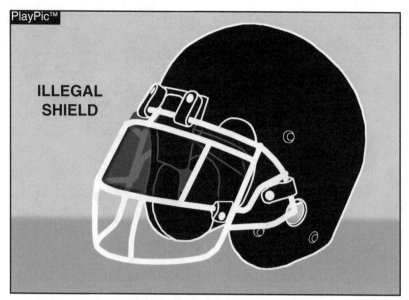

ILLEGAL
SHIELD

1-5-3n If an eye shield is worn, it must be constructed of a molded, rigid material that is clear and permits 100 percent (no tint) allowable light transmission.

1-5-4 Prior to the game, the referee and umpire must visit each team. The head coach is responsible for verifying to the referee in the presence of the umpire that all his players are legally equipped and in compliance with the rules. The umpire will examine and determine legality of any questionable player equipment.

1-6-2 Players are allowed to use Local Area Network (LAN) phones and headphones during authorized conferences conducted in front of their team box and within 9 yards of the sidelines.

1-6-2 An authorized conference in front of the team box can be conducted as far onto the field as the 9-yard marks. Regardless if the conference takes place between the inbounds lines or within the 9-yard marks in front of the team box, a coach may use LAN phones or headphones.

Rule 2

Definitions of Playing Terms

Coaches and officials have a tendency to overlook Rule 2, thinking that definitions are not as important as, for example, those situations dealing with various types of rules infractions and their respective penalties. Nothing could be further from the truth. Rule 2, indeed, is the most important rule in the book. A few examples of some basic definitions:

1. Batting is intentionally slapping or striking the ball with the arm or hand.

2. A catch is the act of establishing player possession of a live ball in flight.

3. Force is not a factor when a backward pass or fumble is declared dead in the end zone of the opponent of the player who passed or fumbled, with no player possession.

4. A fumble is any loss of player possession other than by legal kick, passing or handing.

5. The line of scrimmage for each team is a vertical plane through the point of the ball nearest the team's goal line.

6. The neutral zone is the space between the two free-kick lines during a free-kick down and between the two scrimmage lines during a scrimmage down.

A–refers to the offensive team that puts the ball in play during a scrimmage down. B–refers to their opponents, the defensive team. K–refers to the kicking team, while R–identifies the receiving team during a free or scrimmage kick. The offense is the team which is in possession. At such time, the opponent is the defense.

To fully understand the game, everyone concerned must have a complete understanding of the definitions. The definitions are clear and concise. Terms used in the definitions are unique and actually form the language of the game.

2-3-2a This is a legal blocking position with closed or cupped hands. The hands are in advance of the elbows and not extended more than 45 degrees from the body. The elbows may be either inside or outside the frame of the shoulders. The hands are closed or cupped with the palms not facing the opponents. The forearms may not be extended more than 45 degrees from the blocker's body. If they are, the hands must be open and shall not be locked.

2-3-2b This is a legal blocking position with extended arms and open hands. Team A blockers may use open hands when blocking if the hands are in advance of the elbows and within the blocker's frame and the opponent's frame. The hands must be open when the forearms are extended more than 45 degrees from the blocker's body.

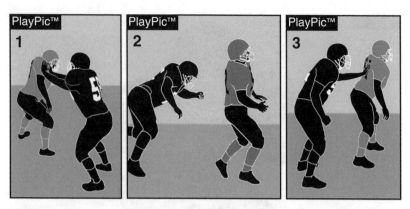

2-3-2b, 2-5-2 The PlayPics depict contact outside the free-blocking zone. The original contact in (1) is legal (2-5-2). However, the opponent evades the blocker in (2). The blocker makes illegal contact on the back in (3). The block was not continuous and results in a block in the back foul in (3). If the blocker had maintained contact in (2) the block would have been legal.

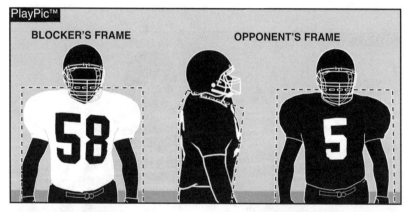

BLOCKER'S FRAME   OPPONENT'S FRAME

2-3-2b (2 & 3) The frame of the blocker's body is the front of the body at or below the shoulders. The frame of the opponent's body is at the shoulders or below, other than the back.

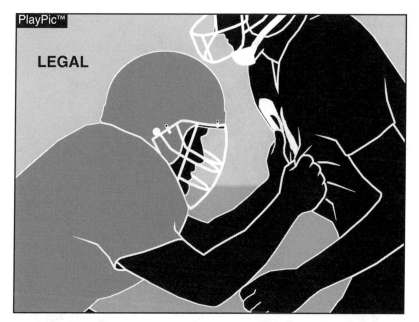

LEGAL

2-3-5b Any defensive player may use hands to get to a runner or loose ball as long as such contact is not pass interference, a personal foul or illegal use of hands.

2-3-7 When the blocker's initial contact is with the opponent's hands, the block is considered to be above the waist, even though subsequent contact is below the waist. The player being blocked can generally protect himself against significant lower-leg contact if he has his hands on the blocker during initial contact.

2-3-7 If the blocker has made initial contact above the waist from the front or side and in continuation slides down and makes contact below the waist, the block is legal. The point of the initial contact in (1) determines whether it is above or below the waist.

2-3-8 While the free-blocking zone exists, simultaneous high-low blocks (1) and simultaneous low-low blocks (2) in the free-blocking zone are not chop blocks and are legal.

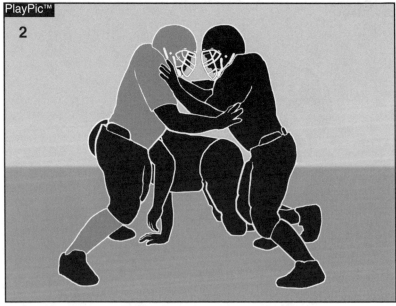

2-3-8 The defensive player is engaged with the offensive player, who is blocking high (1). When the second offensive player throws a delayed low block (2), it is a chop block.

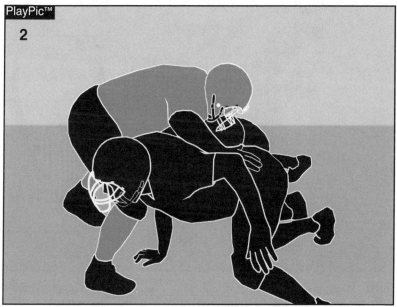

2-3-8 The defensive player is engaged with the offensive player, who is blocking low (1). When the second offensive player throws a delayed low block (2), it is a chop block.

2-4-1 When the contact by an opponent causes an eligible receiver who is airborne to first contact the ground out of bounds, the pass is ruled complete if the covering official judges the receiver would have landed inbounds had there been no contact. This is a completed pass. To complete a catch, the airborne player must maintain possession of the ball when he returns to the ground.

2-4-1 No catch. The receiver does not have possession of the ball inbounds when he comes down. When there is possession, the first foot to touch the ground determines whether it is a catch — as it must touch inbounds, even if the other foot then touches out of bounds. If the feet touch the ground simultaneously, both must be inbounds.

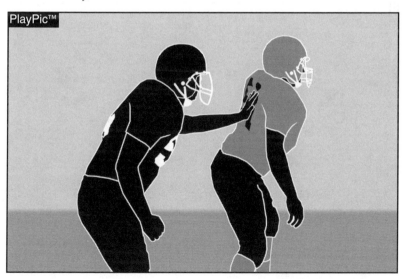

2-5-2 Blocking in the back is against an opponent with the initial contact inside the shoulders, below the helmet and above the waist. The penalty for blocking in the back is 10 yards.

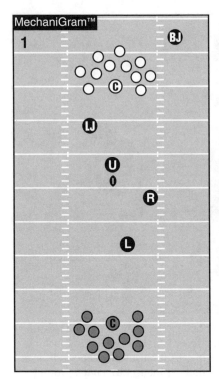

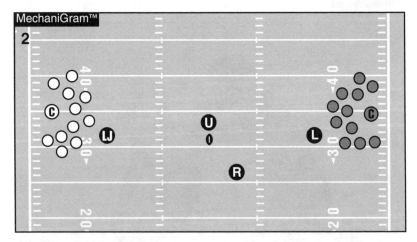

2-6-2 Two types of authorized conferences are permitted. In (1) a coach may confer with the 11 players between the inbounds lines; (2) one or more team members and coaches may confer directly in front of the team box within 9 yards of the sideline; (3) if a coach-official time-out is granted for the review of a possible misapplication of a rule only one coach is permitted to confer with the referee in the vicinity of the sideline (3-5-11).

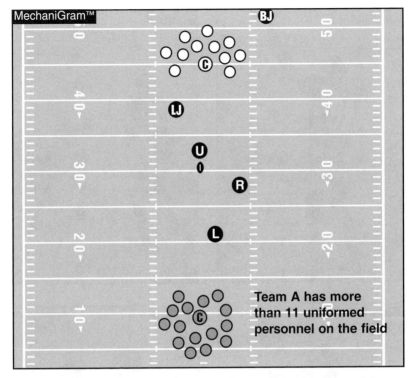

Team A has more
than 11 uniformed
personnel on the field

2-6-2b It is illegal to have more than 11 players meet with the coach for a conference between the inbounds marks. The penalty is 15 yards (9-8-1f).

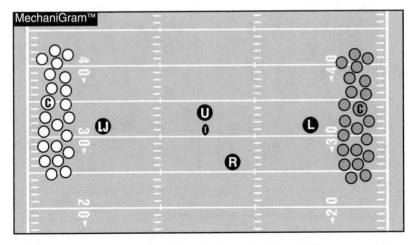

2-6-2 For a time-out conducted within 9 yards of the sideline, any number of team members and coaches may participate.

2-9-1 The prohibition against contacting a player who has given a valid fair-catch signal ceases if the kick is muffed. When No. 80 catches the ball in (4), it is a fair catch. The contact in (3) is ignored unless unnecessarily rough or flagrant. The captain may choose to snap or free kick anywhere between the inbounds lines on the yard line through the spot of the catch.

2-9-4 A signal given after the kick has touched a receiver or after it has touched the ground is an invalid fair-catch signal. The ball becomes dead as soon as the kick is caught or recovered. The foul will be enforced as a post-scrimmage kick foul.

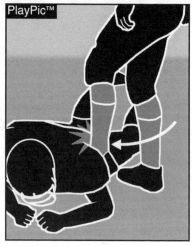

2-11 Fighting is any attempt by a player or nonplayer to strike or engage an opponent in a combative manner unrelated to football. Included are attempts to strike with hand(s), arm(s), leg(s), feet or foot, whether or not there is contact. The four examples of fighting pictured all call for a 15-yard penalty and disqualification.

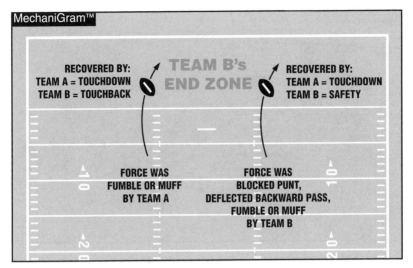

RECOVERED BY:
TEAM A = TOUCHDOWN
TEAM B = TOUCHBACK

TEAM B's END ZONE

RECOVERED BY:
TEAM A = TOUCHDOWN
TEAM B = SAFETY

FORCE WAS
FUMBLE OR MUFF
BY TEAM A

FORCE WAS
BLOCKED PUNT,
DEFLECTED BACKWARD PASS,
FUMBLE OR MUFF
BY TEAM B

2-13-1 Force is the result of energy exerted by a player which provides movement of the ball. A new force may result from a fumble, kick or backward pass which has been grounded. Force is a factor only when it concerns the goal line and in only one direction — from the field of play into the end zone. On kicks going into R's end zone, force is not a factor since it is a touchback regardless of who supplied the force.

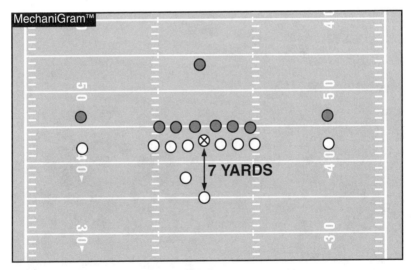

7 YARDS

2-14-2 A scrimmage kick formation is a formation with at least one player seven yards or more behind the neutral zone and in a position to receive the long snap. No player may be in a position to receive a hand-to-hand snap from between the snapper's legs.

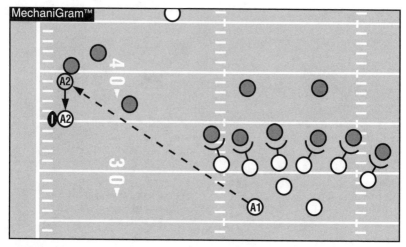

2-15-2 The airborne receiver possesses the pass at the 39-yard line. The defensive contact causes him to be driven backward and the catch is completed well short of the 39. Since the defender caused the change in direction, forward progress is awarded to the farthest advancement after possessing the ball.

B's END ZONE

2-15-2 Airborne receiver No. 5 possesses the ball beyond the plane of B's goal line. The defensive contact forces No. 5 out of the end zone and the catch is completed in the field of play. No. 5 is given forward progress at the point of possession and it is a touchdown.

2-16-2c Any single flagrant foul results in disqualification of the offender. Among the acts that may be considered flagrant are violent and repeated pulls on a face mask (1), intentional contact of an official (2) and prolonged taunting of an opponent (3).

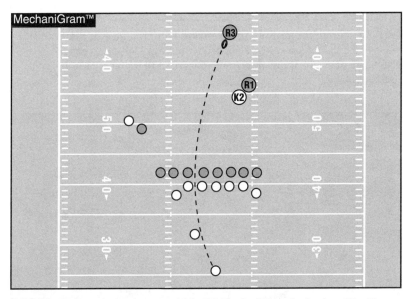

2-16-2h During the scrimmage kick, R1 blocks K2 in the back at R's 45-yard line. The post-scrimmage kick spot is the end of the kick, which is R's 35-yard line.

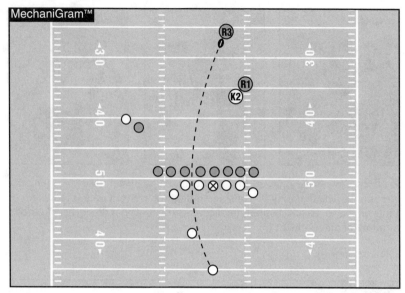

2-16-2h During the scrimmage, K2 grasps R1's face mask at R's 35-yard line as R3 makes a fair catch. The post-scrimmage kick enforcement procedure does not apply on K fouls. This penalty is enforced from the previous spot.

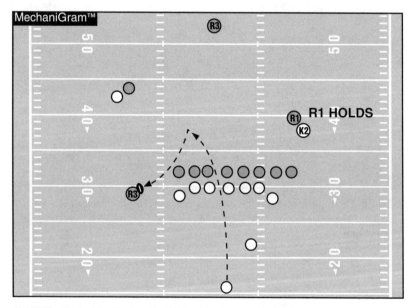

2-16-2h R1 holds during the kick, which is recovered by R3 behind the line. The penalty is enforced from the spot of the foul.

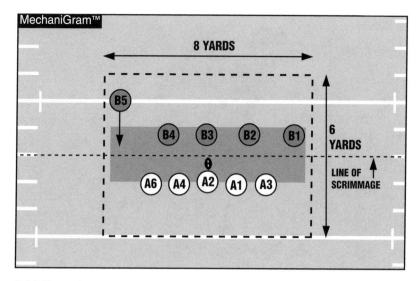

2-17-2 In 11-player football, all players involved in blocking below the waist must be on the line of scrimmage and in the free-blocking zone at snap. Also, the contact must take place in the zone. B5 moves to line of scrimmage just prior to the ball being snapped and therefore meets the definition of a lineman.

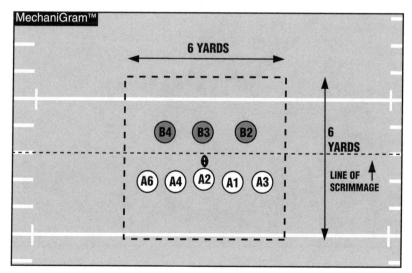

2-17-2 In nine- eight- and six-player football, the free-blocking zone is a square area extending laterally 3 yards either side of the spot of the snap and 3 yards behind each line of scrimmage.

2-18 A fumble (1) is any loss of player possession other than by kick, pass or handing. A fumble may be recovered and advanced by any player of either team. A muff (2) occurs when a player touches a loose ball in an unsuccessful attempt to gain possession.

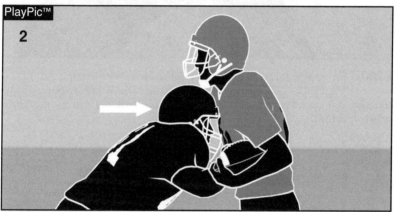

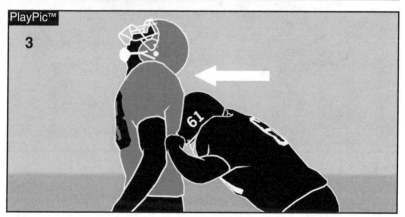

2-20, 9-4-3i, 9-4-3i Note Helmet contact is dangerous and illegal. Butt blocking (1), face tackling (2) and spearing (3) are all fouls carrying a 15-yard penalty.

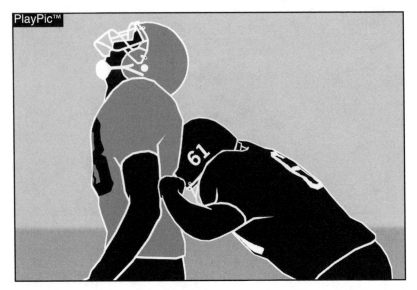

2-20-1c No. 61 is spearing. If the contact is of such severity that it is ruled flagrant, the offender shall be disqualified. The use of the helmet to punish and abuse an opponent cannot be tolerated and the rule declaring it illegal must be strictly enforced.

2-24-4 A legal scrimmage kick is made from in or behind the neutral zone as in (1) and (2). As in a forward-pass play, the down marker can be used as a reference point because it denotes the forward limit of the neutral zone. In (3) it is an illegal kick because the kicker's foot was beyond the neutral-zone plane on contact.

2-25-2 In (1) No. 88 is not on his line because neither his head or foot breaks the plane through the snapper's waist. In (2) No. 88 is legally on the line.

B's END ZONE

2-26-3 A touchdown is scored even though the ball has not penetrated the goal-line plane inside the sideline. Since the runner is touching inbounds when the ball breaks the plane of the goal-line extended, it is a touchdown. However, if the runner is not touching inbounds when the ball breaks the plane of the goal-line extended, it is not a touchdown and the ball is spotted where it broke the sideline plane.

2-31-2 Note The official must rule whether the action illustrated results in a fumble or an incomplete pass. The official is to make his judgement based upon the movement of the passer's arm at contact. If the arm is stationary or moving backward on contact (1), the result is a fumble. If the arm is moving forward on contact (2), the result is an incomplete pass.

2-32-3 Of the offensive players who are not on their line of scrimmage, all except the player under the snapper must be a back. The flanker is not in legal position, because a part of his body is breaking the plane of an imaginary line through the waistline of the nearest lineman, but not the waistline of the snapper.

**K MISSES BALL
R MAKES CONTACT**

**NOT A KICKER,
CONTACT NOT
UNNECESSARILY
ROUGH —
NO FOUL**

2-32-8 A player becomes a kicker when his knee, lower leg or foot makes contact with the ball. When the player in (1) "whiffs" on the kick, he is not considered a kicker. The contact by the opponent only caused the K player to lose his balance and was not unnecessarily rough (2). There is no foul.

PlayPic™

1

KICKER STARTS TO RUN

PlayPic™

2

KICKER STOPS AND KICKS; R MAKES CONTACT

2-32-8 A player becomes a kicker when his knee, lower leg or foot makes contact with the ball. In (1), the K player is a runner, not a kicker. It is the defensive player's obligation by rule to avoid illegal contact. The official must judge if the defender had reasonable opportunity that a kick would be made.

2-39 It is a shift when the quarterback goes from his position in (1) to his presnap position in (2). The movement of his head and/or shoulders in (2) is not a shift, but would be a false start if it simulated the start of a play. After assuming the position in (2), the quarterback and the other players of A must be simultaneously stationary for at least one second before the snap or before a player goes in motion.

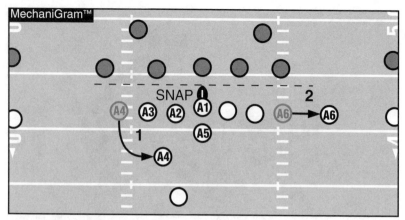

2-39 Whether the movement in (1) and (2) is simultaneous or is done individually, it is a shift. It is a shift whether the movement is to the line, from the line or along the line. The movement of one or more A players to a new position is a shift. It is also a shift when the offensive team moves from the huddle or a player(s) goes from an upright or hands-on-knees position to a down position. Following a shift, all Team A players must be simultaneously set for at least one second before the snap or before a player goes in motion.

Rule 3

Periods, Time Factors and Substitutions

The clock running time for high school football games is 48 minutes, divided into four 12-minute periods. Between the second and third periods, there is an intermission of 15 minutes followed immediately by a three-minute interval for required warm-up activity preceding the beginning of the third period. With proper notification, the intermission may be extended to a maximum of 20 minutes. The opposing coaches may agree to reduce the intermission to a minimum of 10 minutes.

Periods may be shortened in any emergency by agreement of the opposing coaches and the referee. By mutual agreement of the opposing coaches and the referee, any remaining period may be shortened at any time or the game terminated. When weather conditions are considered to be hazardous to life or limb of the participants, the crew of officials is authorized to suspend the game. An official's time-out is authorized when heat/humidity may create a health risk for players.

Obvious errors in timing may be corrected by the referee if discovery of the error is made prior to the second live ball following the error, unless the period has officially ended. No other adjustment in timing is authorized.

The rules are extremely liberal insofar as substitutions are concerned. There are seven possible violations:

1. When a substitute enters during the live-ball period.
2. When a player who has been replaced is not off the field before the ball becomes live.
3. When a substitute enters the game and is then replaced or a replaced player re-enters as a substitute during the same dead-ball period unless during that interval, there was acceptance of a penalty, a dead-ball foul, a charged time-out or the end of a period.
4. When a replaced player, or a substitute who was unable to complete a substitution does not leave the field on the side of his team box.
5. When a replaced player does not leave the field immediately.
6. When an entering substitute is not on his team's side of the neutral zone at the snap.
7. When a replaced player, player or substitute leaves the field opposite the side of his team box.

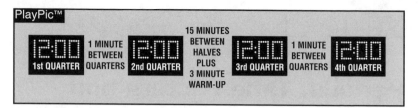

3-1-1 The normal 15-minute period between halves may be extended by state association approval to a maximum of 20 minutes upon proper notification at least five minutes prior to scheduled kickoff. By mutual agreement of the coaches, the halftime intermission may be reduced to a minimum of 10 minutes. The head coach is responsible for his team being on the field for the mandatory warm-up at the end of the intermission.

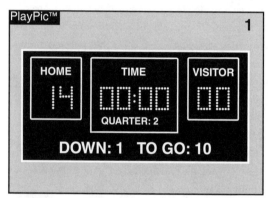

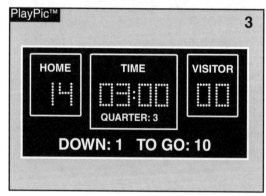

3-1-1 Immediately after the halftime intermission expires (1), the referee must signal the timer to put 3 minutes on the clock (2) and to immediately start the clock for the mandatory warm-up period.

3-1-5 When weather conditions are determined to be hazardous to life or limb of the participants, the crew of officials is authorized to delay the start or suspend the game. Interrupted games shall be continued from the point of interruption, unless the teams agree to accept the existing score as final, or there are conference, league or state association rules which apply.

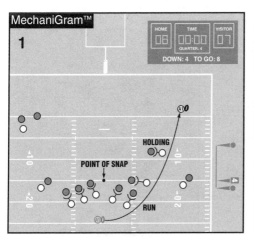

3-3-3a Since the offensive holding foul in (1) occurred during the last timed down of a period, the period will be extended with an untimed down if the penalty is accepted. If the penalty is declined, the touchdown is scored and the period is over following the try. An unsportsmanlike foul or a nonplayer foul is not considered when determining if a period is to be extended because such penalty is automatically enforced from the succeeding spot. An untimed down is indicated by using the signal in (2).

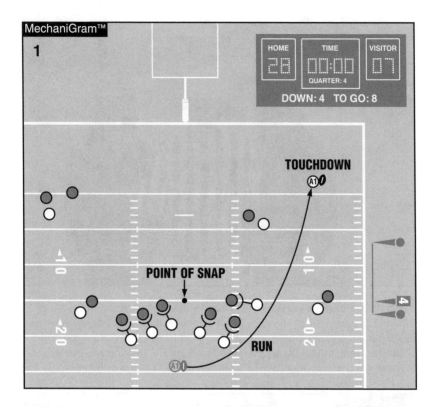

MechaniGram™

1

HOME **28** TIME **00:00** QUARTER: 4 VISITOR **07**

DOWN: 4 TO GO: 8

TOUCHDOWN

POINT OF SNAP

RUN

3-3-3d In (1), a touchdown is scored during the last down of the fourth period. The winner of the game has already been determined. In (2) the referee gives the signal to indicate the game is ended. The try is waived unless the potential point(s) is necessary or required as part of the state association's play-off qualification system.

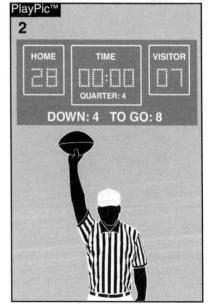

PlayPic™

2

HOME **28** TIME **00:00** QUARTER: 4 VISITOR **07**

DOWN: 4 TO GO: 8

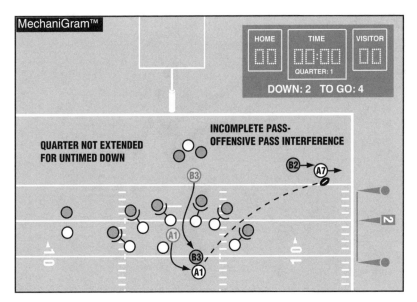

3-3-4b Offensive pass interference occurred on this incomplete pass during the last timed down of a period. The period will be not extended with an untimed down if the penalty is accepted. An unsportsmanlike foul or a nonplayer foul is not considered when determining if a period is to be extended because such penalty is enforced from the succeeding spot.

3-3-5 This foul by B is a dead-ball foul. All dead-ball fouls after the end of the first half are enforced on the third period kickoff. If a dead-ball foul occurs after time has expired for any period, the penalty is measured from the succeeding spot. This succeeding spot could be the sunsequent kickoff or the start of an overtime period.

3-4-1a During a kickoff or any other free kick (1), the clock will not be started until the ball is touched, other than first touching by K. When K touches the ball beyond the neutral zone, as in (2), the clock is started (3). When K secures possession, the ball becomes dead and the clock is stopped. K may not advance the ball. The recovery by K results in a first down for K.

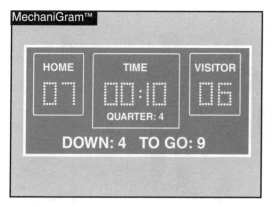

3-4-3i If the penalty is accepted for a delay-of-game foul, the clock shall start with the snap. A number of specific situations constitute delay of game, however, any conduct which unduly prolongs the game is delay.

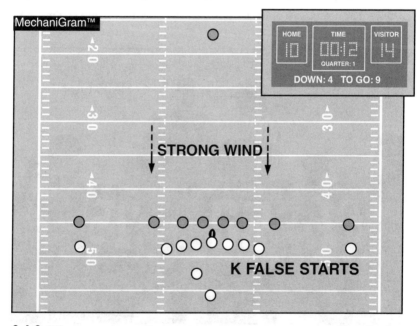

3-4-6 Whenever a team attempts to conserve or consume time illegally, the referee shall order the clock started or stopped. The kicking team tried to consume time and fouled to keep from kicking into the wind. By altering the normal timing procedure, no advantage can be gained because the clock will not start until the snap.

3-5-2a The head coach or the head coach's designee may request a time-out.

3-5-4 Successive charged time-outs may be granted each team during a dead-ball period provided the team has time-outs remaining. Each team is entitled to three during each half. Unused time-outs from the first half cannot be used in the second half or in overtime. Unused second half time-outs may be utilized in overtime if allowed by state association rules. No single charged time-out shall exceed one minute. When a team has used its allowable time-outs in each half, its coach and captain should be notified. A time-out may not be shortened unless both teams are ready to play.

3-5-7e It is an officials' time-out whenever a request is made for a designated injured player who is then required to leave the field for at least one down. The player must leave the game for one down, even if his team subsequently takes a charged time-out in this situation. It is illegal participation if the injured player does not stay out for at least one down unless the halftime or an overtime intermission occurs prior to the next down.

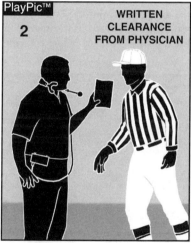

WRITTEN CLEARANCE FROM PHYSICIAN

3-5-10b A player who is injured is determined to be unconscious in (1). The officials are responsible for making the determination. The referee may or may not be aided by other crew members or by team-box personnel in making the determination. Such a player may not return without written authorization of a physician (M.D./D.O.), as seen in (2).

3-5-10c When an official discovers a player who is bleeding, has an open wound, has any amount of blood on his/her uniform, or has blood on his/her person, he shall stop the clock or delay the ready-for-play signal. The player must leave the game for at least one down under provisions of the apparently injured-player rule. The bleeding must be stopped, the wound covered, the uniform and/or body appropriately cleaned and/or the uniform changed before returning to competition.

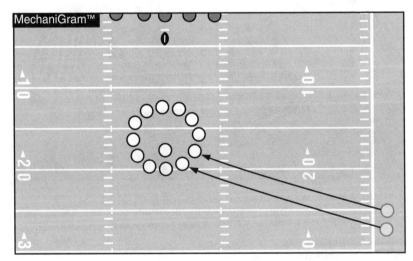

3-7-2 Two substitutes come onto the field and enter the huddle. No one leaves. This is a dead-ball foul for illegal substitution. Replaced players are required to leave the field immediately.

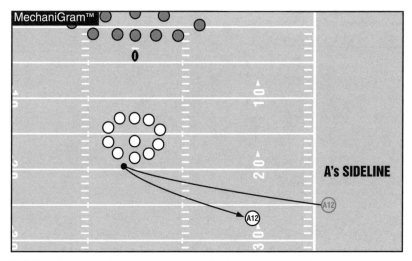

3-7-2 A player, replaced player or a substitute who is unable to complete the substitution is required to leave the field at the side on which his team box is located.

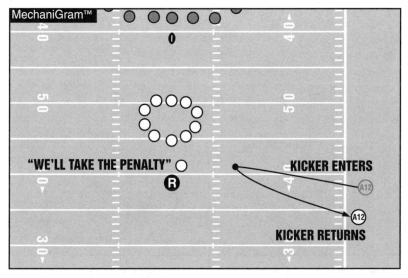

3-7-3 Following a third-down play, a substitute for Team A enters the field for an apparent punting situation. However, a foul has occurred during the down and Team A accepts the penalty. The substitute who previously entered is allowed to return to his team box since the penalty acceptance cancels the unwanted substitution.

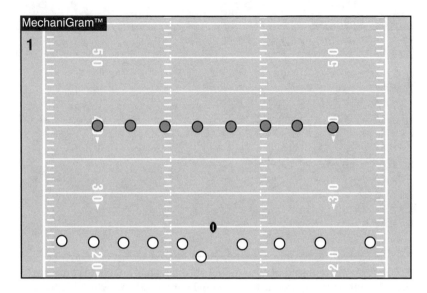

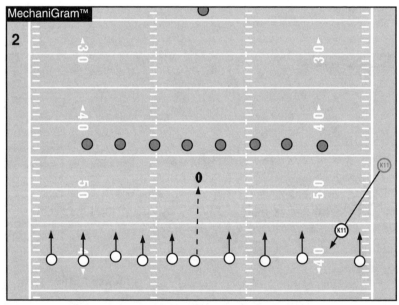

3-7-5 In (1), K has 10 players on the field. Although K11 is in the neutral zone after the ball has been declared ready (2), it is not encroachment. An entering substitute is not a player for encroachment purposes until he reaches his team's side of the neutral zone. Since the ball is kicked with K11 in the neutral zone, the ball is live and it is an illegal-substitution foul for not being on his team's side of the neutral zone when the ball is kicked.

Rule 4

Ball in Play, Dead Ball and Out of Bounds

There are two ways to put the ball in play, with a free kick or with a snap. The ball remains dead and a down is not begun if a snap or free kick is attempted before the ball is ready for play, or there is an illegal snap or other snap infraction. Each half is started with a kickoff. A kickoff also puts the ball in play after a successful field goal and following a try. A free kick follows a safety and if chosen, following a fair catch or awarded catch. The ball becomes dead and the down is ended:

1. When a runner goes out of bounds or his forward progress is stopped.
2. When a live ball goes out of bounds.
3. When a forward pass (legal or illegal) is incomplete.
4. When a legal kick breaks the plane of R's goal line, unless a field goal is scored.
5. When a loose ball is on the ground and no player attempts to secure possession.
6. When a loose ball is simultaneously caught or recovered by opposing players.
7. When a loose ball is touched by or touches anything inbounds other than a player, substitute, official, the ground, etc.
8. When the kickers catch or recover any free kick.
9. When the kickers catch or recover a scrimmage kick beyond the neutral zone.
10. When prior to any touching by R, the kickers touch a scrimmage kick beyond the neutral zone after it has come to rest.
11. Following a valid or invalid fair-catch signal when the kick is caught or recovered by R.
12. When a touchdown or field goal is scored.
13. During a try when B secures possession or it is apparent the kick will not score.
14. When the helmet comes completely off a player in possession of the ball.
15. Whenever an official sounds a whistle inadvertently.

When the ball goes out of bounds, the out-of-bounds spot is fixed by the yard line through the ball's foremost point. When a runner goes out of bounds, the inbounds spot is fixed by the yard line through the foremost point of the ball at the time the runner crosses the plane of the sideline.

4-2-2 Exc. 2 The ball remains live if the holder rises and catches or recovers an errant snap (1) and immediately returns his knee(s) to the ground (2) and places the ball for a kick (3) or again rises to advance, hand, kick or pass (4).

4-2-2 Exc. 2 The snap in (1) is errant. The ball remains live if the holder rises and catches or recovers an errant snap and immediately returns his knee(s) to the ground (2) and places the ball for a kick or again rises to advance, hand, kick or pass (3).

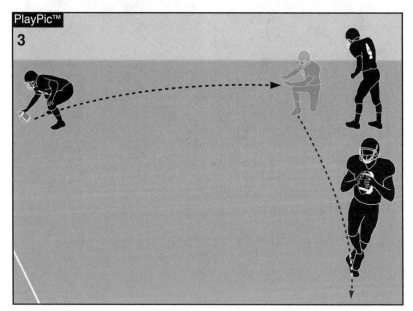

4-2-2a Exception No. 4 is in position to kick and the holder has a knee(s) on the ground at the snap in (1). The exception to the basic dead-ball rule is in effect when both these conditions are being met at the snap. The ball remains live for a kick as in (2), or if the holder rises with the ball (3) to run, pass or drop kick.

4-2-2a Exception A holder with his knee(s) on the ground who has a teammate in position to kick at the snap as in (1), is allowed to rise to catch or recover an errant snap. The ball remains live if he goes to his knee(s) immediately after catching or recovering the snap. The holder is then allowed in (3) or (4) to do what he could have done if the snap had been accurate and he had not risen from his knee(s) to begin with. If the snap is muffed or the holder fumbles, he may recover with his knee(s) on the ground and place the ball for a kick or he may rise with it.

BACKWARD PASS

4-2-2e The backward pass is not caught in (1). When opposing players simultaneously possess a backward pass, as in (2), the ball becomes dead immediately. This ball belongs to the passing team.

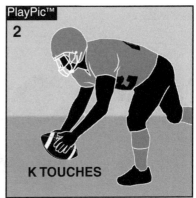

4-2-2f When a scrimmage kick rolls to a complete stop (1) and it is touched by K (2), the covering official will immediately sound his whistle to indicate the ball is dead. In (3) the R player is advancing with a dead ball. Touching by K of a scrimmage kick at rest is not first touching.

4-2-2k The covering official shall sound his whistle immediately when the helmet comes completely off a player who is in possession of the ball. The down counts and the ball belongs to the team at the spot it became dead.

4-2-3b The inadvertent-whistle procedure is the same for action in (1), (2) and (3). If the ball is loose and the whistle sounds following an illegal kick, fumble, illegal forward pass or backward pass, the team last in possession may take the results of the play where possession was lost or replay the down. In (1) or (3), if the penalty is accepted, the administration of the foul takes precedence over the inadvertent whistle.

4-3-1 In (1), since the receiver possesses the free kick before he touched out of boundswith the ball inside the sideline plane, he is considered to have caused the ball to be out of bounds. The ball will be put in play at the inbounds spot on the 14-yard line. In (2), since there was no touching by R prior to the player being out of bounds, K has caused the free kick to go out of bounds. R may either put the ball in play from the inbounds spot, put the ball in play 25 yards beyond the previous spot, or have the 5-yard penalty enforced against the kicking team from the previous spot and kick off again.

1

RUNNER HIT BY TACKLER

2

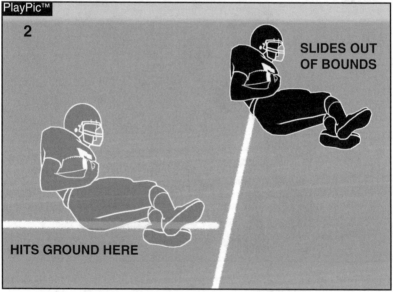

SLIDES OUT OF BOUNDS

HITS GROUND HERE

4-3-2 The runner is inbounds when he is hit by an opponent (1). The ball is dead when the runner hits the ground (2). Even though the runner slides out of bounds, the ball has not been out of bounds and the clock continues to run. The ball is placed at its forward point where the ball became dead. The runner is down when any part of his person, other than hand or foot, touches the ground.

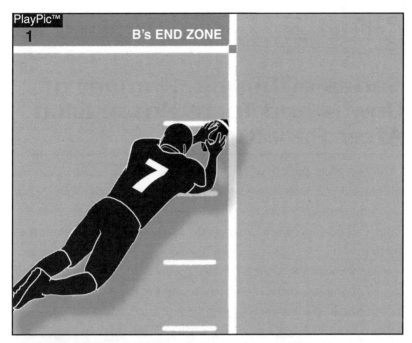

4-3-3 A ball in player possession is out of bounds when the runner or the ball touches anything, other than another player or game official, which is on or outside the sideline or end line. The spot where the ball becomes dead is under the foremost point of the ball in possession of the runner when he crosses the plane of the sideline at B's one-yard line (1). No touchdown is scored in (2) since the runner was airborne and was not touching inbounds when the ball broke the plane of the goal-line extended.

Rule 5

Series of Downs, Number of Downs and Team Possession After Penalty

The team which puts the ball in play by scrimmage after a free kick, touchback or fair catch, is awarded a series of four consecutively numbered downs in which to advance the ball to or beyond the line to gain. A new series is awarded if the ball belongs to the offensive team on or beyond the line to gain. It is also a new series and the ball will belong to the defensive team at the end of any down, if B gained possession during that down, or at the end of a fourth down, if the offensive team was in possession behind the line to gain. If a receiver is the first to touch a scrimmage kick while it is beyond the neutral zone, a new series will be awarded to the team in possession at the end of the down, unless the penalty is accepted for a non post-scrimmage kick foul which occurred before the kick ended.

When a penalty is declined, the number of the next down is the same as if the foul had not occurred. When a foul by A (or K) or B (or R) occurs during a scrimmage down and before any change of team possession, and before a receiver is first to touch a scrimmage kick while it is beyond the neutral zone, the ball belongs to A (or K) after penalty enforcement. The number of the next down is the same as that of the down during which the foul occurred unless acceptance of the penalty carries an automatic first down or loss of down, or the penalty enforcement or advance results in a first down. The loss of down aspect of a penalty has no significance following a change of possession or if the line to gain is reached after enforcement.

When a foul by A or B occurs prior to a scrimmage down, or simultaneously with the snap, the number of the next down after enforcement is the same as the number established before the foul occurred, unless enforcement for a foul by B results in a first down. After a distance penalty, the ball belongs to the team in possession at the time of the foul. Team possession may then change if a new series is awarded.

1. R TOUCHES

2. K HOLDS

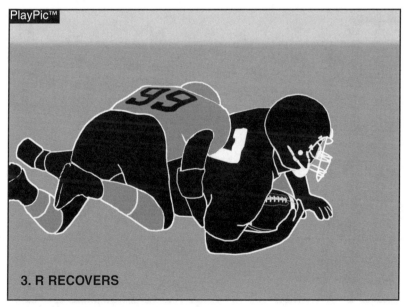

3. R RECOVERS

5-1-3d R may choose to decline the penalty and take the results of the play and keep the ball at the spot of recovery. If they accept the penalty for the holding foul, K will replay the down after enforcement from the previous spot. The foul occurred during a loose-ball play.

1. R TOUCHES

2. R HOLDS

3. K RECOVERS

5-1-3f The series is not ended if K accepts the penalty for the foul during a loose-ball play as the penalty is enforced from the previous spot and the down is replayed. In this play, K will undoubtedly take the results of the play, decline the penalty and take the ball at the spot of recovery.

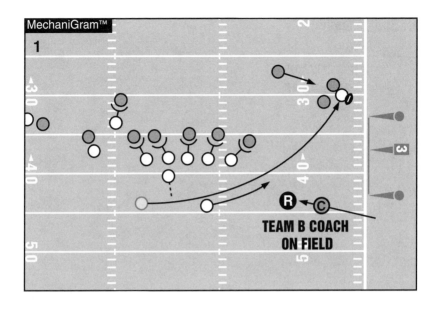

TEAM B COACH
ON FIELD

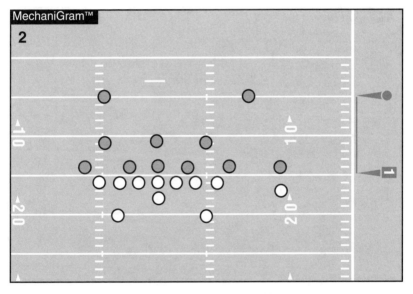

5-3-1 When a new series is gained as in (1), the penalty for the unsportsmanlike foul is administered before the line to gain is established. In (2), the chain and box are then set, making it first and 10 for Team A.

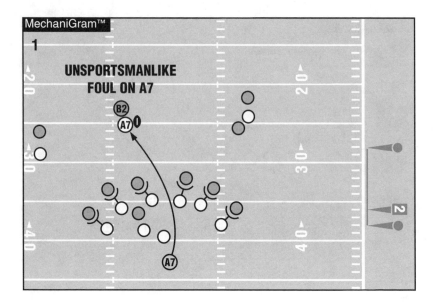

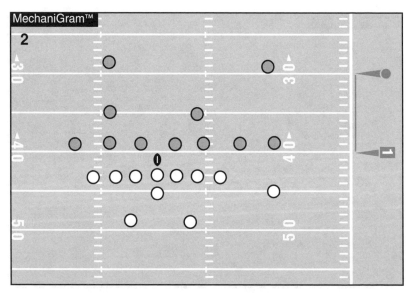

5-3-1 Team A gains a first down, but A7 commits an unsportsmanlike foul after the down in (1). Since the foul occurred prior to the subsequent ready-for-play signal, the line to gain is established following penalty enforcement. It is first and 10 for Team A in (2).

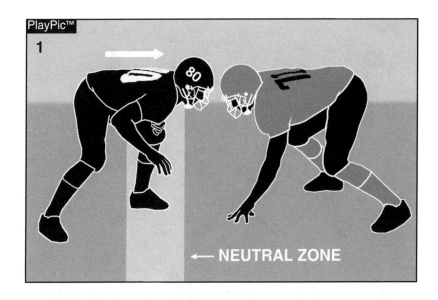

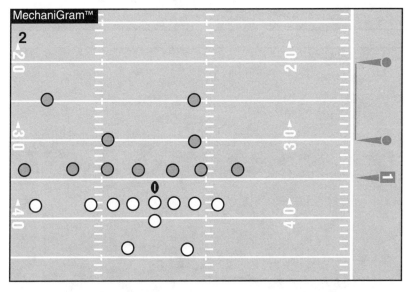

5-3-1 Following the ready-for-play signal on first down, No. 80 encroaches (1). It is first and 15 for Team A following penalty administration (2). A foul after the ready is the only situation where it will be more than first and 10 for Team A to start a new series.

5-3-1 Team A is short of the line to gain on a fourth-down play, which dictates it is a new series for Team B. The penalty for the dead-ball illegal personal contact seen in (1) is enforced before the chain and box are set for B's series. It is first and 10 for Team B at B's 35-yard line (2).

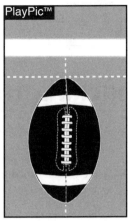

| **BALL IS DEAD IN THIS POSITION** | **DETERMINE FORWARD POINT** | **PLACE AT FORWARD POINT** |

5-3-2 Whenever a measurement is required, the ball shall be placed with its long axis parallel with the sideline before measurement. If it is a first down, the referee gives the signal, spots it and marks it ready for play. If the line to gain has not been reached, the referee signals the distance needed to both sides.

Rule 6

Kicking the Ball and Fair Catch

A free kick is used to put the ball in play to start a free-kick down. A free-kick line is established for each team and is always 10 yards apart. If not moved because of a penalty, K's free-kick line for a kickoff is its 40-yard line, its 20-yard line for a kick following a safety, and the yard line through the spot of the catch following a fair catch.

The offensive team may punt, drop kick or placekick from in or behind the neutral zone before team possession has changed. Such a kick is a scrimmage kick. When any member of the kicking team touches a scrimmage kick between the goal lines and beyond the neutral zone, before it is touched by a member of the receiving team and before the ball has come to rest, it is first touching. First touching does not cause the ball to become dead.

Any receiver may signal for a fair catch while any kick is in flight. Any receiver who gives a valid or invalid fair-catch signal is prohibited from blocking until the kick has ended.

If any receiver gives a valid signal for a fair catch and he catches the free kick in or beyond the neutral zone and between the goal lines, or catches the scrimmage kick beyond the neutral zone and between the goal lines, it is a fair catch and the ball becomes dead. Only the receiver who gives a valid signal is afforded protection and only where a fair catch may be made. If, after a receiver gives a valid signal, the catch is made by a teammate, it is not a fair catch but the ball becomes dead. Following a valid or invalid signal by the receiving team, the ball becomes dead when caught or recovered by any receiver.

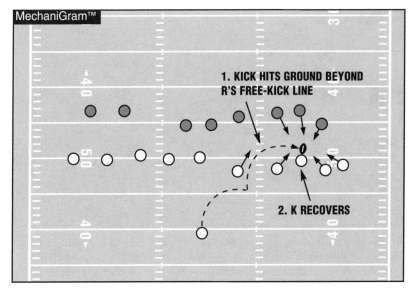

1. KICK HITS GROUND BEYOND R'S FREE-KICK LINE

2. K RECOVERS

6-1-5 If the free kick has gone beyond the plane of the receiver's free-kick line and has touched the ground, any K player may then recover. Both conditions must be met — has touched the ground and has gone beyond the plane. The order of occurrence has no bearing on the fact that K may then recover. K may not advance a recovered kick.

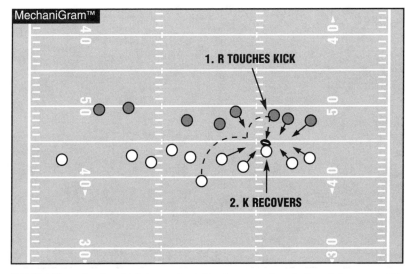

1. R TOUCHES KICK

2. K RECOVERS

6-1-5 When the free kick is touched first by a receiver before it has gone 10 yards, it may be recovered by any K player. The recovery causes the ball to become dead and the down is ended. No K player may advance the recovered kick. However, it is a first down for K.

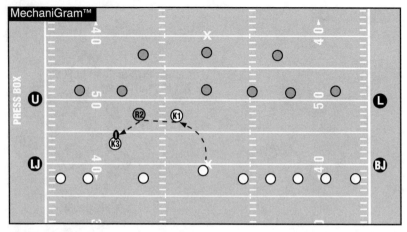

6-1-5 K1's muff in the neutral zone on a free kick causes the ball to touch R2 and K3 recovers. Because R2's touching was caused by K1's muff, the touching by R2 is ignored as they will decline first touching. It will be R's ball at the spot of K3's recovery.

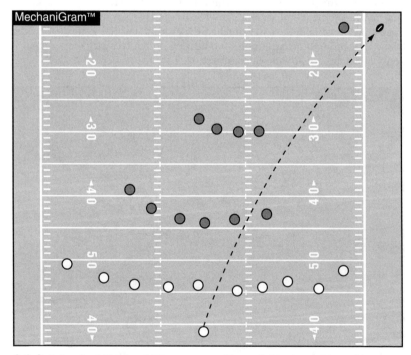

6-1-8 It is a foul if a free kick goes out of bounds between the goal lines, and it was not touched by R. R may decline the penalty and take the ball at the inbounds spot or 25 yards from the previous spot, or accept the 5-yard penalty and have K rekick.

6-1-9 R's No. 80 muffs the kick. There is no recovery by K as No. 5 first contacts the ground out of bounds. R will put the ball in play at the inbounds spot.

6-2-3 When a field-goal attempt fails, it is treated like any scrimmage kick and the ball remains live until the down ends. Since K recovered behind the neutral zone, they may advance. Officials must be alert and not confuse a field-goal attempt with a try. When it is apparent there will be no score from a kick try, the down is ended.

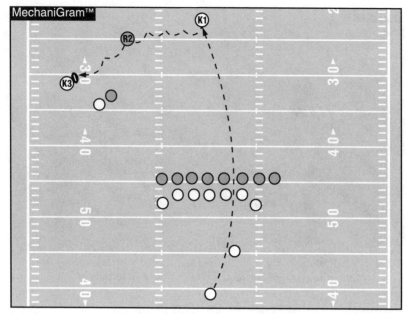

6-2-4 K1 legally bats the scrimmage kick, which deflects off R2. The loose ball is recovered by K3. Because R2's touching was caused by K1's bat, the touching is ignored. R may take the ball at the spot of K3's recovery.

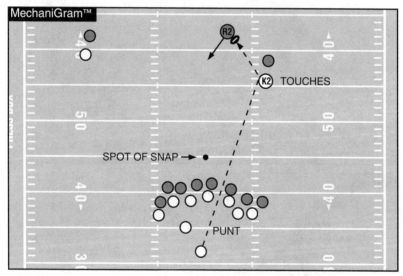

6-2-5 First touching by the kicking team does not cause the ball to become dead. This is a legal advance. The right of R to take the ball at the spot of first touching by K is canceled if R touches the kick and thereafter commits a foul or if the penalty is accepted for any foul committed during the down.

6-2-6 The neutral zone is expanded up to a maximum of 2 yards during a scrimmage down. No. 70 has touched a low scrimmage kick in the expanded neutral zone. The touching of a low scrimmage kick by any player is ignored if the touching is in or behind the expanded neutral zone.

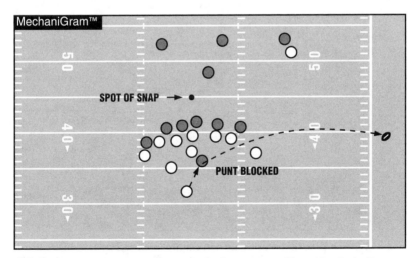

6-2-7 When the blocked scrimmage kick goes out of bounds, the ball belongs to the receiving team at the inbounds spot. This is true regardless of the down and distance when the scrimmage kick was made or where it went out of bounds between the goal line.

END ZONE

6-3-1 When a potential scoring kick in flight is touched by R in his end zone, it does not become dead if the ball thereafter passes through the goal. The field goal counts. It would also count if the ball touched the crossbar or uprights and deflected through the goal. If R jumps up and blocks the kick away from the goalposts, it causes the ball to become dead immediately; and, on a field goal, it is a touchback.

6-5-1 This is a legal block by R's No. 36 even though R's No. 80 may not advance if the kick is caught or recovered as a valid fair-catch signal was given. However, No. 80 may not block until the kick ends because he has signaled.

6-5-6 Kick-catching interference. The receivers have the option of taking the results of the play, accept an awarded fair catch at the spot of the foul, or replaying the down after having the distance penalty enforced from the previous spot.

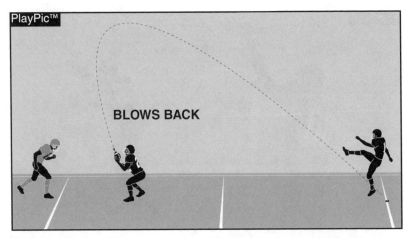

BLOWS BACK

6-5-6 It is kick-catching interference when the kickers touch a free kick in flight. It makes no difference whether or not the ball has been beyond the receiver's free-kick line. This restriction ends after a receiver touches the kick. R may choose an awarded fair catch at the spot of the foul with no distance penalty or have the distance penalty enforced from the previous spot and rekick.

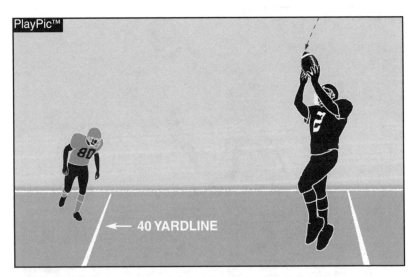

← 40 YARDLINE

6-5-6 Exception A member of the kicking team legally catches a scrimmage kick beyond the neutral zone. This is only permissible when no member of the receiving team is in position to catch the ball. There is no requirement that the receiver must make or attempt to make a catch — only that he is in position where he could make a catch if he desired.

6-5-6 Exception In this situation, two receivers are in position to attempt a catch. The opponent commits kick-catching interference. The ball becomes dead with the catch. R may take the ball at the spot of the catch or have the penalty enforced from the previous spot and the down replayed. The receivers must be given an unmolested opportunity to catch the kick.

6-5-6 Exception The punt in flight hits another K player in the shoulder as he goes downfield to cover the kick (1). A receiver is in position to make a catch (2). It is kick-catching interference. R may accept an awarded fair catch at the spot of the foul or accept the penalty of 15 yards from the previous spot and a replay of the down. K's recovery (3) is negated.

6-5-6 Exception This is a legal play. The kickers may touch, bat or muff a grounded kick even if an R player is in position to make the catch. The receivers may take the results of the play or the ball at the spot of first touching by K.

Rule 7

Snapping, Handling and Passing the Ball

For any scrimmage down, the ball may only become live with a legal snap. A snap is the legal act of passing or handing the ball from its position on the ground in a quick and continuous backward motion of the hand(s) during which the ball immediately leaves the hand(s). A snap ends when the ball touches the ground or a backfield player before it touches a Team A lineman.

The snap begins when the snapper first moves the ball other than in adjustment. The snapper is allowed to make certain preliminary adjustments while not changing the location of the ball. These preliminary movements may be made, but both hands may not be taken off the ball once the snapper has placed a hand(s) on the ball.

After the ball is ready and before the snap, each player of Team A must momentarily be within inside the 9-yard marks before the ball is snapped. Not more than one A player may be in motion at the snap and then only if such motion is not toward B's goal line. After a huddle or shift, all players of A must come to a stop and remain simultaneously stationary for at least one second before the snap.

A forward pass may be thrown only by the team which has put the ball in play from scrimmage, provided the ball is released with both feet of the passer in or behind the neutral zone. There may be only one legal forward pass during a down. During a pass, the ball travels in flight, that is, is thrown rather than handed forward.

During a forward pass, there are at least five ineligible receivers. On a pass which goes beyond the neutral zone, ineligibles may not go beyond the neutral zone before the pass is in flight. Ineligibles may go downfield if the pass does not go beyond the expanded neutral zone. When a forward pass is touched by a defensive player, all A players become eligible immediately.

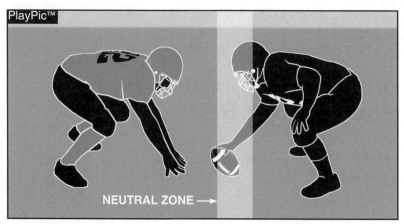

NEUTRAL ZONE →

7-1 A scrimmage down is started with a snap. The snapper's feet must be behind the neutral zone. His head may be in the neutral zone, but not beyond the foremost point of the ball. The ball may be preliminarily adjusted after which the snapper may not make a movement that simulates a snap. The snapper may not remove both hands once he has placed a hand(s) on the ball after the ready-for-play. The snap must be one continuous backward motion in which the ball immediately leaves the hand(s) of the snapper and must touch a Team A non-lineman or the ground before it touches a Team A lineman.

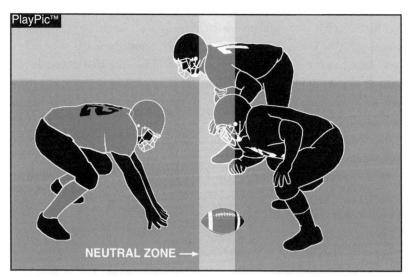

NEUTRAL ZONE →

7-1-6 Encroachment restrictions are not in effect for those in the neutral zone as the snapper has not placed a hand(s) on the ball. The players who are in the neutral zone may move and be out of the neutral zone before the snapper puts his hand(s), on the ball. Before the snapper places his hand(s) on the ball it is encroachment for any other player to touch the ball or an opponent or be in the zone to give defensive signals. All other encroachment restrictions begin after the ready-for-play when the snapper places his hand(s) on the ball.

7-1-7a When the quarterback "chucks" his hands under the center (1) or bobs his head (2), it simulates snap action and is a false start. Jerky movements which simulate the beginning of the down or acts clearly intended to cause B to encroach are false starts. These acts must be judged on their own merits rather than whether or not B encroaches.

7-2-3 If the ball is snapped, this would be an illegal formation foul at the snap. Of the A players who are not on their line at the snap, only one player may penetrate through the waistline of his nearest teammate who is on the line, and he must be in position to receive the snap, even though he is not required to receive it.

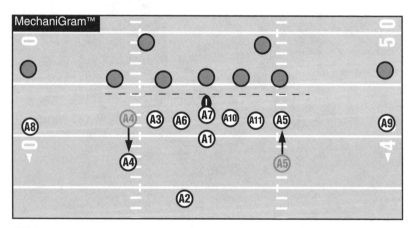

7-2-6 The movement of one or more offensive players to new set positions is a shift. This formation is legal. A3 is now on the end of the line; if he is also wearing an eligible receiver's number, he is an eligible receiver. A9 is also on the end of the line and is eligible if he is wearing an eligible receiver's number. Following a shift, all 11 players must simultaneously meet the one-second motionless requirement prior to the snap.

7-5-2b The passer has one foot beyond the plane of the neutral zone when he releases the ball on a forward pass. The pass is illegal. An illegal forward pass is part of a running play with the end of the run being the spot from which the pass is thrown.

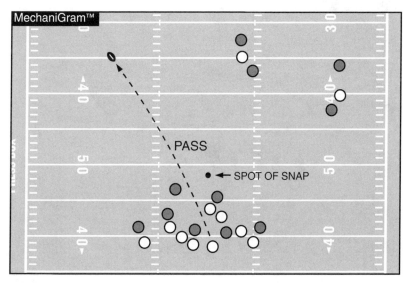

7-5-2c This is an illegal forward pass as it was intentionally thrown into an area not occupied by an eligible offensive receiver. If the referee judges it was also done to conserve time, he shall start the clock on the ready. If accepted, the penalty is enforced from the end of the run — the spot of the pass.

7-5-2d Exception The illustration shows how the quarterback stops the clock legally. Following the hand-to-hand snap, the ball is immediately thrown forward to the ground as he steps backward to clear himself from the line play.

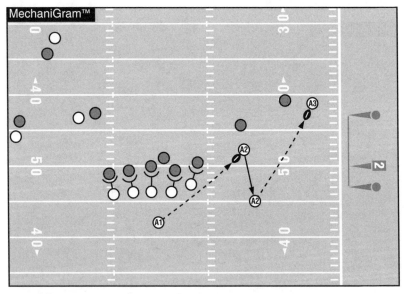

7-5-2e A1 throws a pass to A2 who is beyond the line of scrimmage. A2 retreats behind the line of scrimmage and then throws a pass to A3. The pass by A2 is an illegal pass as only one forward pass be thrown.

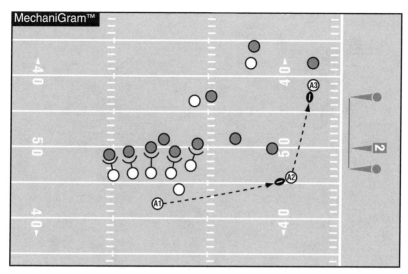

7-5-2e A1 throws a forward pass to A2 who throws second to A3. The pass by A2 is an illegal pass.

LINE OF SCRIMMAGE

7-5-7 Pass interference restrictions apply only beyond the neutral zone and only if the legal forward pass, untouched by the defense in or behind the neutral zone, crosses the neutral zone. The touching by No. 61 makes No. 60 an eligible receiver.

7-5-8a, 7-5-10 During a down in which a legal forward pass crossed the neutral zone, a Team A receiver may not contact an opponent with his hands beyond the neutral zone for any purpose until the pass has touched a player. If a forward pass is thrown beyond the neutral zone, the contact results in offensive pass interference. Team A restrictions begin with the snap.

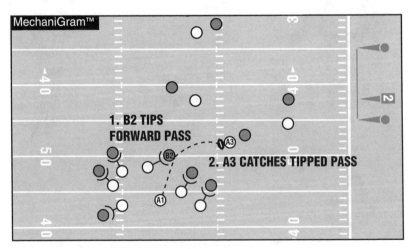

7-5-9, 7-5-10 Tipped pass behind the line of scrimmage by B. Lineman A3 is eligible as the pass was tipped by B behind the line of scrimmage. Pass restrictions for both A and B ended when B touched the pass.

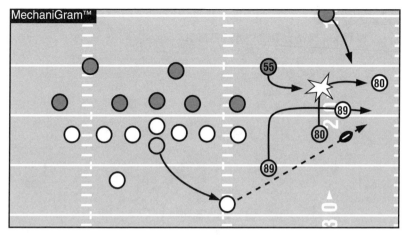

7-5-10a The contact by No. 55 constitutes defensive pass interference. No. 80 is entitled to his position and is entitled to maintain that position on the field. Defensive pass interference carries a 15-yard penalty, plus an automatic first down.

7-5-10b Defensive pass interference. No. 28 has directed his attention to blocking the vision of the receiver which indicates an intent to hinder the receiver rather than catch or bat the ball and it is, therefore, interference even if there is no contact.

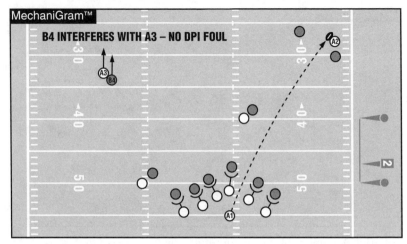

7-5-11 A foul or contact away from the direction of the pass is not pass interference. However, this does not take away the restrictions on illegal use of hands, holding, or a personal foul.

7-5-11a When two opposing eligible pass receivers are making a simultaneous and bona fide attempt to catch or bat the ball, and there is unavoidable contact, it is not a foul. The defender and receiver both have a right to attempt to gain possession of the pass.

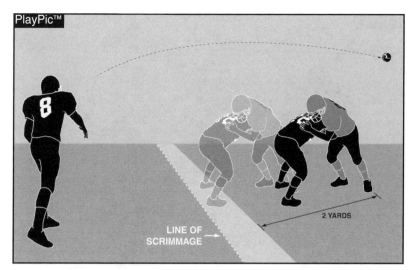

7-5-12 An ineligible receiver may block an opponent who is within 1 yard of his line of scrimmage at the snap and drive him back up to 2 yards into the defensive secondary. The neutral zone is expanded to this extent during a forward pass which crosses the neutral zone. If the defensive player is not on his line of scrimmage at the snap, it is pass interference to contact him downfield.

7-5-12 Ineligible receiver downfield and illegal touching by No. 60 because he was beyond the neutral zone before the legal forward pass which crossed the neutral zone was thrown. On a pass that crosses the neutral zone, touching by A does not make the ineligible receivers eligible.

7-5-12 Ineligible No. 71 is not downfield illegally, due to the fact No. 61 touched the ball prior to the legal forward pass crossing the neutral zone.

Rule 8

Scoring Plays and Touchback

Anytime a live ball, in the possession of a runner, penetrates the plane of the opponent's goal line or touches the goal line, it is a touchdown. It is also a touchdown when a player gains possession of a live ball in his opponent's end zone.

Following a touchdown, the scoring team is entitled to a try from the opponent's 3-yard line. During the try, a successful field goal will score one point and two points will be scored if a scrimmage play results in what would normally be a touchdown. One point will be scored if the play results in what would normally be a safety in B's end zone. The try is waived if the touchdown is scored during the last down of the fourth period and the outcome of the game has been decided and the point(s) is not required for playoff qualification.

A safety is scored when a player gives the ball the force or impetus that carries it across his own goal line, and it becomes dead there not in possession of its opponents. It is also a safety when a player on offense commits any foul for which the penalty is accepted and measurement is from a spot in his end zone.

A field goal is scored when a player drop kicks or placekicks the ball from scrimmage or from a free kick after a fair catch or awarded catch, so that the ball passes above the crossbar and between the vertical uprights of his opponent's goal.

It is a touchback when any kick (except a successful field-goal attempt) breaks the plane of R's goal line or if a forward pass which is intercepted in B's end zone becomes dead there in B's possession. A fumble, muff or bat of a backward pass or fumble, results in a touchback when the force or the new force which sends the ball to or across the opponent's goal line is provided by the offensive team and the defense is in team possession, or the ball is out of bounds when it becomes dead on or behind the goal line. If any kick becomes dead on or behind the kicker's goal line with the ball in possession of the kicking team and the new force was a muff or a bat of the kick by the receiver after it touched the ground, it is a touchback.

8-2-1 It is a touchdown whenever the live ball, in possession of a runner, breaks the vertical plane of the opponent's goal line, regardless of whether or not the runner is in contact with the ground. The position of the runner's body is of no consequence as long as the ball in his possession breaks the vertical plane of the goal line.

8-2-1a Touchdown. The pass is completed in the end zone before the receiver goes out of bounds. To complete a catch, an airborne player must have the ball in his possession when he first returns to the ground inbounds or be contacted by an opponent who prevents him from doing so.

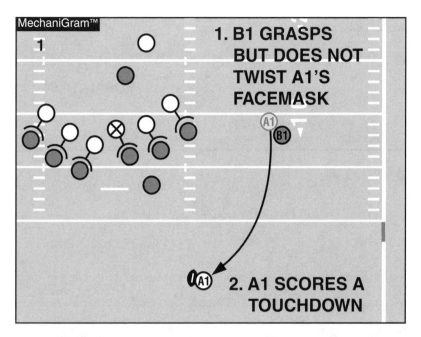

1. B1 GRASPS BUT DOES NOT TWIST A1'S FACEMASK

2. A1 SCORES A TOUCHDOWN

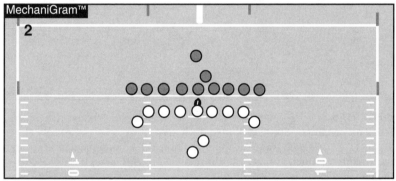

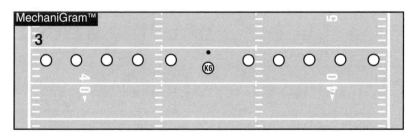

8-2-2 A team that is fouled during a play that results in a touchdown (1) may choose to have the penalty for a live-ball foul enforced on the try (2) or the subsequent kickoff (3).

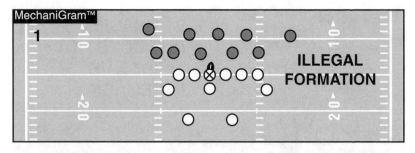

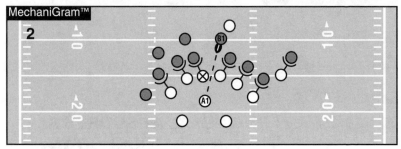

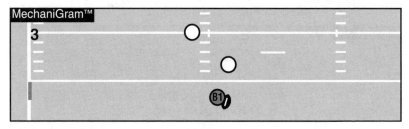

8-2-3, 10-5-3 If the foul is by A before B gains possession and then scores, B has no penalty options, as it must decline A's foul to keep the score (10-5-3). In (1), A is flagged for an illegal formation. A1's pass intercepted (2) and returned for a touchdown (3). If B wants to keep the score, it must decline the penalty. There is no option for enforcement on the subsequent kickoff.

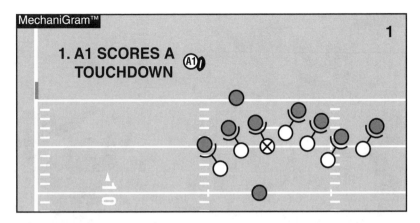

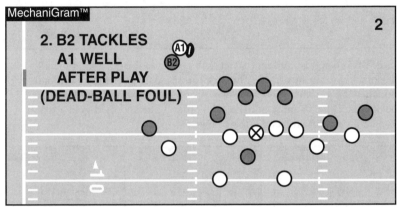

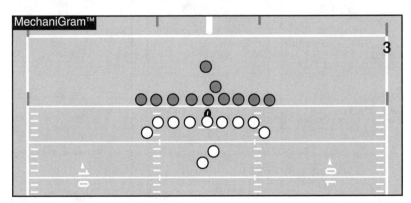

8-2-2 The optional penalty enforcement does not apply on dead-ball fouls. In (1), A1 scores a touchdown. Several seconds after the play is over, B2 contacts A1 (2). Because that is a dead-ball foul A's only option is to have the penalty enforced from the succeeding spot, in this case, the try (3).

8-3-2b When it is apparent a kick will not score during a try, the ball becomes dead immediately. The kick cannot score after the kicked ball touches the ground. There's no way A or B can score any points once the kick fails. Officials must be aware that after a blocked field-goal attempt, which is not a try, the ball remains live.

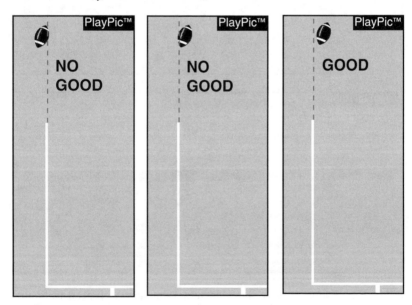

8-4-1 During a field-goal attempt, the kick must pass above the crossbar and between the vertical uprights or the inside edges of the uprights extended in order to be successful. If any part of the ball penetrates the plane of the inside edges of the vertical-uprights extended, it is unsuccessful.

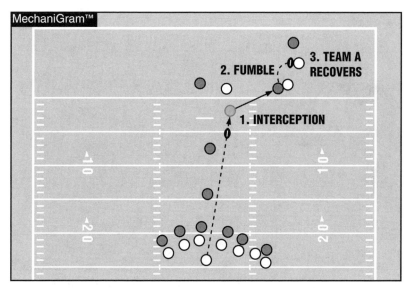

8-5-2a Exception The Team B player intercepts (1). His original momentum carries him into his own end zone after a catch inside his 5-yard line. If the fumble is recovered by Team A in Team B's end zone (3), it is a touchdown for Team A.

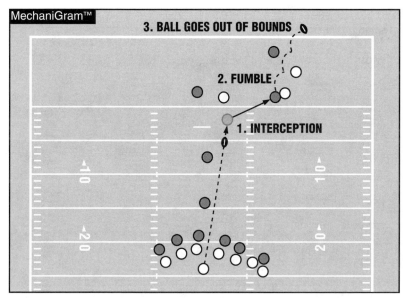

8-5-2a Exception The Team B player intercepts (1). His original momentum carries him into his own end zone after a catch inside his 5-yard line. If the fumble goes out of bounds behind the goal line (3), it belongs to Team B on the yard line on which it was intercepted.

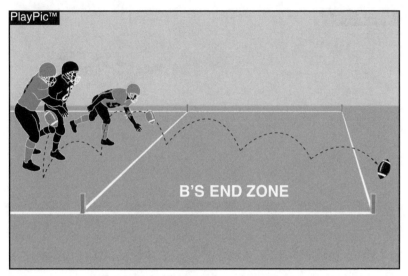

8-5-2b After a fumble has been grounded, a new force may result from a muff or bat. If the covering official rules B's attempted recovery provided a new force causing the ball to go into and through his own end zone, the result is a safety. If B had not added a new force, A's fumble through B's end zone would have been a touchback.

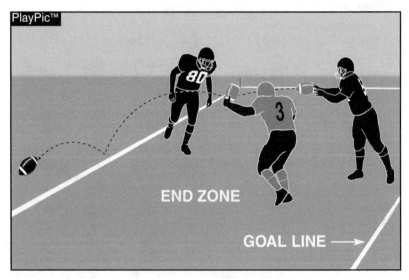

8-5-2b The result of this play is a safety. The force which puts the ball through the end zone is the backward pass. No. 3 did not supply a new force as the backward pass was still in flight when he contacted it.

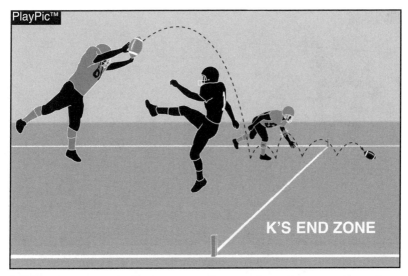

K'S END ZONE

8-5-2b One receiver blocks the punt and the ball is rolling near the goal line when a teammate touches the ball in an attempt to recover. The covering official must judge whether the ball could have gone into the end zone without the touch. Since no new force was given, the original force was supplied by the kick and it is a safety if the ball goes out of bounds from the end zone.

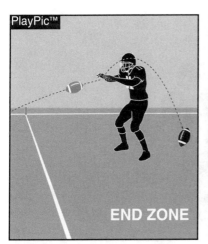

END ZONE

8-5-2c After muffing the snap, No. 11 holds No. 58 to prevent him from recovering the ball. This is a foul by No. 11, for which the penalty is administered toward the end line according to the "all-but-one" principle. The result is a safety. If No. 58 had recovered in the end zone, A's foul could have been declined resulting in a touchdown.

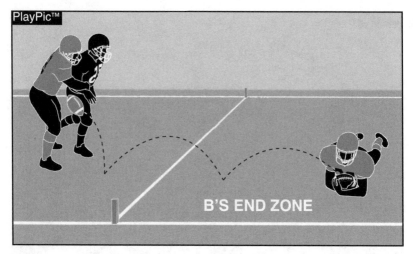

PlayPic™

B'S END ZONE

8-5-3c It is a touchback when a fumble is the force which sends the ball from the field of play across the opponent's goal line and the opponent is in possession in the end zone when the ball becomes dead. If the ball is fumbled through the end zone and out of bounds, it also results in a touchback. If A had recovered in the end zone, it would have been a touchdown.

PlayPic™

END ZONE

8-5-3d A forward pass is the force which causes the ball to cross the opponent's goal line. Following the interception by B, if the ball becomes dead in Team B's possession in the end zone, the result is a touchback. B may run the ball out of the end zone or may down it in the end zone. If B fumbles and A recovers in the end zone, it is a touchdown for A.

Rule 9

Conduct of Players and Others

It must be recognized that participation in sports requires an acceptance of risk of injury. Football is a vigorous, physical contact game and, for this reason, much attention is given to reducing the risk of injury to the players. In addition to requiring player equipment which offers protection, those responsible for administering the program must be certain coaches teach techniques which are within the rules. Officials must accept the responsibility for properly administering the rules as written.

In a game in which forceful, physical contact is not only permitted but encouraged, there will invariably be some injury. However, when injury results from techniques taught for the purpose of physically abusing opponents, such techniques must be eliminated.

Blocking by a player either on offense or defense is legal provided it is not: kick-catching interference; forward-pass interference; a personal foul or prohibited contact such as a chop block, etc. Except to bring down the runner, blocking below the waist is legal only if the player(s) is/are on the line of scrimmage and in the zone at the snap, and the block is in the free-blocking zone. A receiver who gives a valid or invalid signal for a fair catch may not block until the kick has ended.

In order to ensure balance between the offense and defense, definite restrictions are placed upon each. An offensive player is restricted in the use of his hands and arms other than in a legal block. A defensive player may use his hands to push or pull an opponent in order to get at a runner or to ward off a blocker or to reach a loose ball which he may retain following possession. It is always a foul for a player on either team to lock his hands while contacting an opponent with his hands or to strike an opponent with the hand, forearm or elbow.

9-2-3c This contact by No. 61 is not a foul since No. 8 is pretending to be a runner. However, the defensive player must exercise reasonable caution in avoiding any unnecessary tackle. A runner or player pretending to be a runner may be contacted from the front or back.

LINE OF SCRIMMAGE

9-2-3d When No. 80 is no longer a potential blocker, contacting the receiver is illegal use of the hands by the defense. Once No. 80 is on the same yard line as the defender, or after he has made his cut away from the defender, he is no longer a potential blocker. If this contact occurs after a forward pass which crosses the neutral zone is in flight, it is defensive pass interference.

9-3-2 The block is legal, even though contact is below the waist. The restriction on blocking below the waist does not apply unless the opponent had one or both feet on the ground. No. 75 has caused the contact to be below the waist when he jumped in an attempt to block the kick.

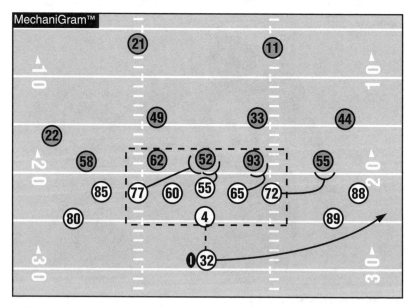

9-3-5a It is legal for offensive linemen to block from behind in the free-blocking zone, provided both players were on their lines of scrimmage and within the zone at the time of the snap and the ball has not left the zone. If the players are on the line of scrimmage but only partially in the zone at the snap, they are considered to be in the zone for purposes of administration.

9-3-5b The offensive blocker is between the runner and the potential tackler. The defender pushes the blocker from behind above the waist, then continues to pursue and make the tackle. The contact by the defender on the blocker is legal. It is also legal to use hands on the back of an opponent when the ball is loose and the player may legally recover it.

9-4-3b The rules provide that it is illegal to contact a player who is clearly out of the play or to make any other contact which is deemed unnecessary and which incites roughness. Also, unwarranted and unnecessary "punishing" of a ball carrier must be eliminated.

9-4-3h Penalty Grasping the face mask or helmet opening is a penalty. If there is twisting, turning or pulling of the face mask or helmet (1), it is a 15-yard penalty; otherwise it is a 5-yard penalty (2). When in doubt, it is a 15-yard penalty.

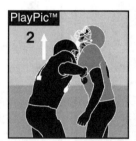

9-4-3i Butt blocking (1 and 2) and face tackling (3) are both tactics which involve initiating contact with the helmet directly into an opponent in blocking or tackling respectively. Both result in a foul for illegal helmet contact.

9-4-3j Striking blows are always illegal. This example of a "clotheslining" tactic by a defensive back must be penalized. The penalty of 15 yards will be measured from the end of the run and the offender shall be disqualified. Tactics such as this have no place in the game.

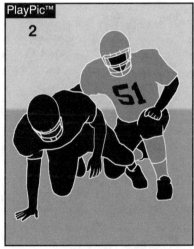

9-4-4 The roughing-the-passer foul by No. 51 carries a 15-yard penalty, plus an automatic first down. The penalty, if accepted, is assessed from the end of the run when it ends beyond the neutral zone and there has been no change of possession.

9-4-4 Penalty After A80's catch (1), the passer is roughed (2). The run ends beyond the neutral zone and the runner fumbles (3). The fumble is recovered by a teammate (4). The roughing penalty is enforced from the spot of the fumble since that is the end of the last run. The spot of the recovery by a teammate is not considered to be another run.

9-4-5 In (1), the R player makes only slight contact with the kicker, which only causes the kicker to spin around (2). The official could judge no foul on this play.

9-4-5 In (1), the R player makes contact with the kicker, which causes the kicker to be displaced (2). This is intended to illustrate running into the kicker.

9-4-5 In (1), the R player contacts the kicker's plant leg, making the kicker extremely vulnerable. The contact knocks the kicker to the ground (2). This is an example of roughing the kicker.

9-4-5 In (1), the kicker takes the snap (1). Another K player blocks an onrushing R player (2). The block causes the R player to contact the kicker (3), knocking him to the ground (4). Because the R player's block caused the contact on the kicker, there is no foul.

9-4-5 A 15-yard penalty is applicable when there is illegal contact on the kicker/holder. The penalty also carries an automatic first down. A bad snap does not automatically eliminate the kicker's protection from roughing.

9-4-7 No defensive player may use the hand(s) to slap a blocker's head (A). In (B), if the slap is to the head while the ball is in the air to pass, it would be defensive pass interference.

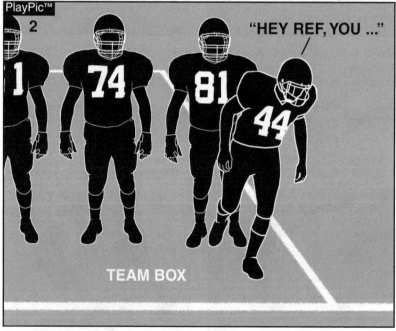

"HEY REF, YOU ..."

TEAM BOX

9-5; 9-8 Penalty No. 44 receives one unsportsmanlike foul as a player in (1) and a second as a non-player in (2). No. 44 is disqualified upon receiving the second unsportsmanlike foul which carries a 15-yard penalty. Officials must keep accurate records of unsportsmanlike fouls.

9-5-1c Players must be penalized for prolonged and excessive acts designed to focus attention on themselves. Such displays must be penalized without hesitation. The unsportsmanlike act is penalized from the succeeding spot.

9-6-1 Team A receiver No. 80 steps on the sideline and then returns inbounds and catches a forward pass. No. 80 has committed an illegal-participation foul. The spot of the foul is the spot where he returned inbounds. No foul if he does not return inbounds. Similar restrictions apply to Team K players.

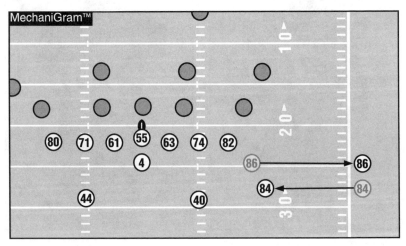

9-6-4c It is illegal participation to use a substitution situation to deceive the opponents at or immediately before a snap or free kick. This act becomes a foul at the snap. If the penalty is accepted, it will be enforced from the previous spot.

R's END ZONE

9-7-2 Exception K may bat a grounded scrimmage kick which is beyond the neutral zone toward his own goal line. This is legal action. If the bat occurred beyond the plane of the goal line, the ball was already dead causing it to be a touchback. K may also bat a scrimmage kick in flight beyond the neutral zone if no R player is in position to catch the ball.

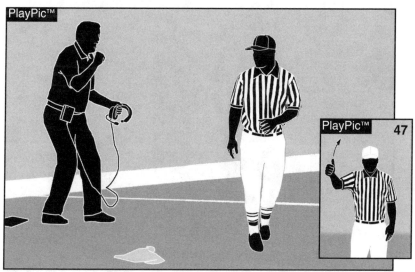

9-8-1 A second unsportsmanlike foul with a 15-yard penalty by the same member of the coaching staff will cause the coach to be disqualified and removed from the stadium area. He may not communicate with coaches or players from the area or from the press box, he may not be in the team locker room during halftime and must adhere to state association rules upon disqualification.

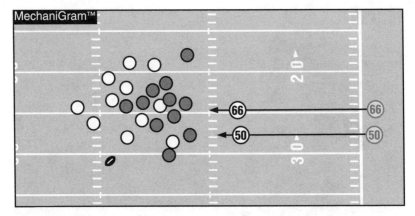

9-8-1l While a fight is taking place on the field, two substitutes of Team A leave their team box and then enter the field. The two substitutes are each charged with an unsportsmanlike conduct foul and are also disqualified. Two 15-yard penalties will be assessed. Substitutes shall not leave the team box during a fight. In addition, the players who are fighting shall be penalized and disqualified.

9-8-3 A maximum of three coaches are allowed to be outside the front of their team box and between the sideline. No other personnel or substitutes are allowed in the coaches' area unless entering or leaving the field. The head coach is responsible for the team box and the coaches' special area.

Rule 10

Enforcement of Penalties

In the NFHS football rules, the penalty-enforcement philosophy is based upon the principle that a team is entitled to the advantage of distance gained without the assistance of a foul. Because of the all-but-one penalty-enforcement principle, it is not necessary to memorize a long list of different rules. It defines a simplified penalty system. If a foul occurs during a down, the basic spot is determined by the type of play. There are two types of plays:

1. A loose-ball play is action during:

   a. a free kick or scrimmage kick

   b. a legal forward pass

   c. a backward pass (including the snap), illegal kick or a fumble made by A from in or behind the neutral zone prior to a change of team possession. A loose-ball play also includes the run (or runs) which precedes such legal or illegal kick, legal forward pass, backward pass or fumble.

2. A running play is any action not included in item 1.

If a foul occurs during a loose-ball play, the basic spot is the previous spot with the exception of post-scrimmage kick fouls. For a running play, it is the spot where the related run ends.

While it is possible to have several running plays during a down, with each one having its own basic spot — where the related run ended — there can be only one loose-ball play, during a down.

If a live-ball foul is followed by a dead-ball foul, the penalty for the live-ball foul will be administered in accordance with the all-but-one principle. The dead-ball foul penalty will then be measured from the succeeding spot. The penalty for any nonplayer or unsportsmanlike foul is administered from the succeeding spot. When there is a double foul during the down, the penalties offset and, in effect, there is no acceptance or declination of them.

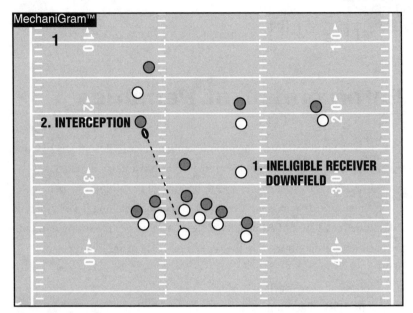

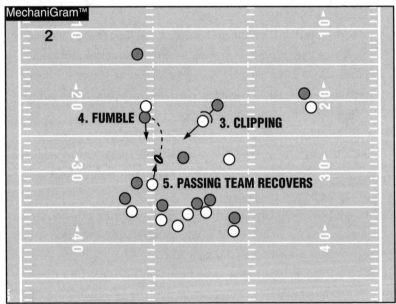

10-2-1b This is a double foul. The team gaining final possession had fouled prior to gaining final possession. The penalties cancel and the down will be replayed from the previous spot. When a double foul occurs, the captains are not consulted since the penalties offset automatically even in those cases where the penalty distances are not the same.

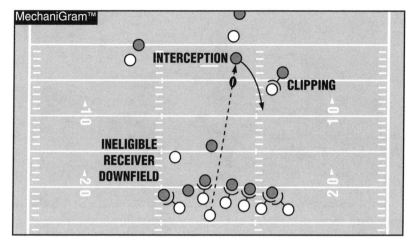

10-2-2 Live-ball fouls by opponents do not always combine to make a double foul. When there is a change of team possession and the team gaining final possession has not fouled prior to gaining possession and declines the penalty for its opponent's foul, that team may retain possession. If B declines the foul for A's ineligible receiver downfield, B will put the ball in play first and 10 following the administration of the penalty for clipping.

FIELD GOAL IS GOOD

10-4 If Team K takes the field goal, the penalty for roughing will be enforced from the succeeding spot. Team K may instead accept the penalty resulting in an automatic first down, plus the distance penalty, which could put them in position to go for a touchdown. If the foul is flagrant, the offender is disqualified whether or not the penalty is accepted.

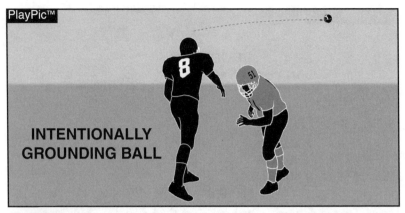

INTENTIONALLY GROUNDING BALL

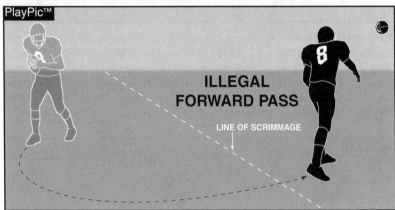

ILLEGAL FORWARD PASS

LINE OF SCRIMMAGE

INTERCEPTS OR CATCHES KICK THEN THROWS FORWARD PASS

10-4-4 Since all illegal forward passes are running plays, the penalty, if accepted in any of these plays, will be enforced from the end of the related run. The down will count unless the forward pass was thrown after a change of possession during the down. Following a change of possession, a loss-of-down penalty has no significance.

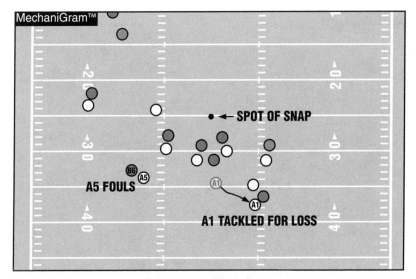

10-4-4 When a foul for offensive holding occurs during a running play and the foul is in advance of the basic spot it is penalized from the basic spot, which is the end of the related run.

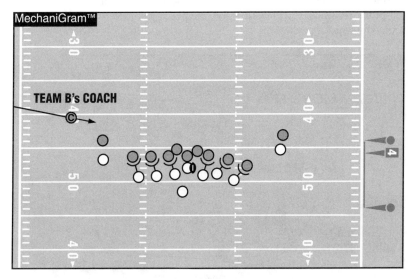

10-4-5a Team A is short of a first down on a fourth-down run. The penalty for the dead-ball unsportsmanlike foul on the Team B coach is administered before the line to gain is established for Team B. It will be first and 10 for B from its own 33-yard line.

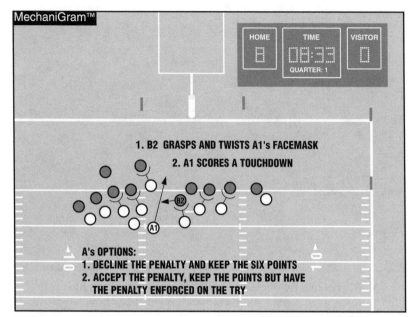

1. B2 GRASPS AND TWISTS A1's FACEMASK

2. A1 SCORES A TOUCHDOWN

A's OPTIONS:
1. DECLINE THE PENALTY AND KEEP THE SIX POINTS
2. ACCEPT THE PENALTY, KEEP THE POINTS BUT HAVE
   THE PENALTY ENFORCED ON THE TRY

10-5-1f, 8-2-2 If a live-ball defensive foul occurs during a touchdown-scoring play when there is no change of possession, the scoring team may accept the results of the play and have the penalty enforced from the succeeding spot.

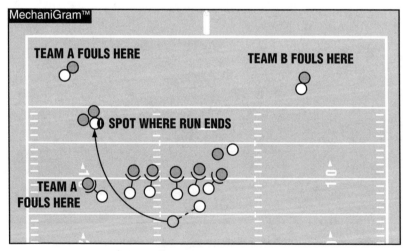

TEAM A FOULS HERE

TEAM B FOULS HERE

SPOT WHERE RUN ENDS

TEAM A FOULS HERE

10-6 Any live-ball foul, other than a nonplayer or unsportsmanlike foul or a foul simultaneous with the snap, is penalized according to the all-but-one enforcement principle. All fouls are penalized from the basic spot, except the foul by the offense which occurs behind the spot. In that case the penalty is administered from the spot of the foul.

NFHS Signal Chart

Ready for play
★ Untimed down

Start the clock

Stop the clock

TV/radio timeout

Touchdown

Safety

Dead-ball foul

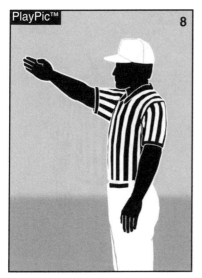

First down

Loss of down

Incomplete pass/unsuccessful try or field goal/ penalty declined/coin toss option deferred

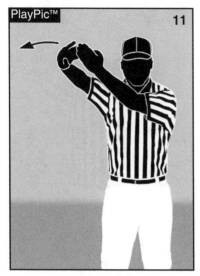

Legal touching

Inadvertent whistle

Disregard flag

End of period

Sideline warning

First touching
Illegal touching

Encroachment

False start
Illegal formation

NOTE: Signal 17 is not depicted because it is an NCAA-only signal

Illegal motion (1 hand)
Illegal shift (2 hands)

Delay of game

Substitution infraction

Equipment violation

Illegal helmet contact

Unsportsmanlike conduct

Illegal participation

Sideline interference
NOTE: Face pressbox when
giving signal.

NOTE: Signals 25 and 26 are for future expansion

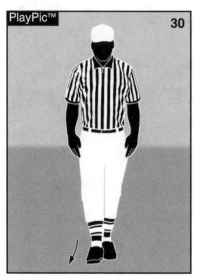

Running into or roughing the kicker or holder

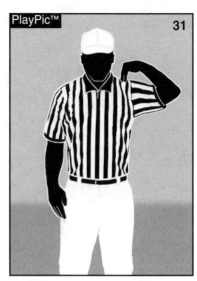

Illegal batting/kicking
(for illegal kicking, follow with point toward foot)

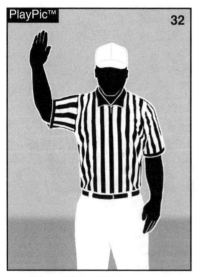

Illegal/invalid fair catch

**Pass interference
Kick-catching interference**

Roughing the passer

Illegal pass
Illegal forward handing
NOTE: Face pressbox when
giving signal.

Intentional grounding

Ineligible downfield on pass

Personal foul

Clipping

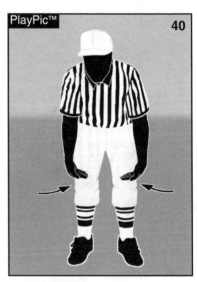

Block below the waist
Illegal block

Chop block

Holding
Obstructing
Illegal use of hands or arms

Illegal block in the back

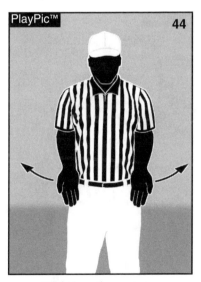

Helping the runner
Interlocked blocking

Grasping of face mask or helmet opening

Tripping

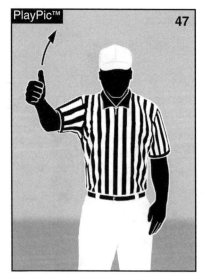

Disqualification

2008 NFHS Football Rules
Penalty Summary

LOSS OF 5 YARDS   **SIGNAL**

Failure to properly wear mandatory player equipment during down 27-23

Delay of game 7-21

Failure to properly wear mandatory player equipment just before snap . . 7-21-23

Illegal substitution 22

Free-kick infraction 7-19

Encroachment 7-18

Free kick out of bounds 19

Invalid or illegal fair-catch signal 32

Snap infraction 7-19

False Start 7-19

Illegal formation 19

Less than seven players on A's line or numbering violation 19

Illegal shift or illegal motion 20

Planned loose-ball infraction 19

Illegally handing ball forward (also loss of down) 35-9

Illegal forward pass (by A) (also loss of down). 35-9

Illegal forward pass (by B). 35

Intentional grounding (also loss of down) 36-9

Ineligible receiver illegally downfield 37

Illegal touching (also loss of down) 16

Helping runner 44

Incidental face mask 45

Running into kicker/holder 30

Sideline interference 7-29

Attendant illegally on field 19

Nonplayer outside of the team box, but not on field 7-29

LOSS OF 10 YARDS

Illegal blocking technique 42

Interlocked blocking 44

Holding 42

Runner grasping a teammate 42

Illegal use of hands or arms 42

Illegal block in the back 43

LOSS OF 15 YARDS

DISQUALIFICATION ASSOCIATED WITH CERTAIN
15-YARD PENALTIES

COACHES-OFFICIALS

MEMBERSHIP INFORMATION

NFHS Coaches Association – NFHS Officials Association

$30.00 ANNUAL DUES INCLUDES

ONE COACH AND ONE OFFICIAL SERVE ON EACH NFHS RULES COMMITTEE!

GENERAL LIABILITY INSURANCE

COACHES' OR OFFICIALS' QUARTERLY SUBSCRIPTION

AWARDS AND RECOGNITION!

➜ JOIN NOW ◄

NOTE: *DO NOT USE FOR CHEER/SPIRIT COACHES - REQUEST NFHS SPIRIT ASSOCIATION FORM FROM ADDRESS BELOW*

Mr/Mrs/Ms: _____ First Name: _____ M.I. _____

Last Name: _____ *(as it appears on your driver's license)*

Home Address: _____This is a new address ☐

City: _____ State/Province _____ Zip _____

Country: _____ Fax: ( ) _____

School/Organization Phone: ( ) _____ Home Phone: ( ) _____

For Insurance Purposes:

Social Security Number _____ Birthdate _____ ☐ Male ☐ Female

E-Mail Address: _____

Primary area of interest/expertise (sport) _____

First Year Officiating _____

First Year Coaching _____

I WORK PRIMARILY IN: *(Check only one)*
☐ High School Sports
☐ College Sports
☐ Youth League Sports

CHECK TYPE OF MEMBERSHIP

☐ **COACH** $30.00

☐ **OFFICIAL** $30.00

(Residents of foreign countries add $9.00 mailing costs)

☐ Check ☐ VISA ☐ MasterCard ☐ American Express

DO NOT MAIL FORM WITHOUT PAYMENT
One annual payment provides member benefits for one year from the date payment is received by the NFHS.

Mail Payment to: NFHS
PO Box 690
Indianapolis, IN 46206

Account No.: _____ – _____ – _____ – _____

Exp. Date: _____ Card Security Code: _____

(call your merchant card provider for location of code.)

Cardholder Name _____

Signature _____

No purchase orders accepted   TOTAL AMOUNT ENCLOSED $_____

NFHS PUBLICATIONS

Prices effective April 1, 2008 — March 31, 2009

RULES PUBLICATIONS

Baseball Rules Book	$6.95
Baseball Case Book	$6.95
Baseball Umpires Manual (2009 & 2010)	$6.95
Baseball Simplified & Illustrated Rules	$7.95
Baseball Rules by Topic	$7.95
Basketball Rules Book	$6.95
Basketball Case Book	$6.95
Basketball Simplified & Illustrated Rules	$7.95
Basketball Officials Manual (2007-09)	$6.95
Basketball Handbook (2008-10)	$6.95
Basketball Rules by Topic	$7.95
Field Hockey Rules Book	$6.95
Football Rules Book	$6.95
Football Case Book	$6.95
Football Simplified & Illustrated Rules	$7.95
Football Handbook (2007 & 2008)	$6.95
Football Officials Manual (2008 & 2009)	$6.95
Football Rules by Topic	$7.95

Girls Gymnastics Rules Book & Manual	$6.95
Ice Hockey Rules Book	$6.95
Boys Lacrosse Rules Book	$6.95
Soccer Rules Book	$6.95
Softball Rules Book	$6.95
Softball Case Book	$6.95
Softball Umpires Manual (2008 & 2009)	$6.95
Spirit Rules Book	$6.95
Swimming, Diving & Water Polo Rules Book	$6.95
Track & Field Rules Book	$6.95
Track & Field Case Book	$6.95
Track & Field Manual (2009 & 2010)	$6.95
Volleyball Rules Book	$6.95
Volleyball Case Book & Manual	$6.95
Wrestling Rules Book	$6.95
Wrestling Case Book & Manual	$6.95

MISCELLANEOUS ITEMS

NFHS Statisticians' Manual	$6.50
Scorebooks: Baseball-Softball, Basketball, Swimming & Diving, Cross Country, Soccer, Track & Field, Gymnastics, Volleyball, Wrestling and Field Hockey	$10.95
Diving Scoresheets (pad of 100)	$7.00
Volleyball Team Rosters & Lineup Sheets (pads of 100)	$7.00
Libero Tracking Sheet (pads of 50)	$7.00
Baseball/Softball Lineup Sheets - 3-Part NCR (sets/100)	$8.50
Wrestling Tournament Match Cards (sets/100)	$7.00
Flipping Coin	$5.50
NFHS Pin	$3.00
Competitors Numbers (Track and Gymnastics – Waterproof, nontearable, black numbers and six colors of backgrounds	
Numbers are 1-1000 sold in sets of 100	$13.00/set
Lane Numbers (1-8), size 4" x 2 1/2"	$7.00/set

MISCELLANEOUS SPORTS ITEMS

High School Sports Record Book (2008)	$12.95
Court and Field Diagram Guide	$19.95
NFHS Handbook (2008-09)	$9.00
Let's Make It Official	$5.00
NFHS NEWS Binder	$9.50

Guide for College-Bound Student-Athletes and Their Parents	$2.00
High School Activities — A Community Investment in America	$79.95

2008-09 NFHS ORDER BLANK

Name_____ Phone _____

School and/or Organization _____

Address _____

| City | State | Zip |

(No PO Boxes. If charging order to a credit card please use address on card.)
If address has changed in the last year please fill in old address.

_____

| Street | City | State | Zip |

Check one of the following: ☐ Visa ☐ MasterCard

Account No. _____ - _____ - _____ - _____ Exp. Date_____

Signature _____

P.O. # _____ (Order totals $50 or more)
(attach P.O.)

Item#	Description	Quantity	Unit Price	Total

SHIPPING & HANDLING CHARGES: If your subtotal is:

$10.00 to $15.00 ....add **$7.95**	$75.01 to $100.00 ...add **$15.95**
$15.01 to $25.00 ....add **$8.95**	$100.01 to $250.00 .add **$18.95**
$25.01 to $50.00 ....add **$9.95**	$250.01 to $500.00 .add **$21.95**
$50.01 to $75.00 .....add **$12.95**	Over $500.01 add 5% of subtotal

Second Day = Standard shipping charges plus **$15.00**
Overnight = Standard shipping charges plus **$25.00**
All shipments to Alaska, Hawaii, Virgin Islands and Canada – add **$10.00**
Call for charges outside continental U.S.
Minimum purchase on each order $10.00 before shipping charges

Subtotal _____

Shipping & Handling Charge _____

TOTAL _____

Send to: **NFHS CUSTOMER SERVICE**
PO Box 361246, INDIANAPOLIS, IN 46236-5324
Phone 800-776-3462, Fax 317.899.7496 or online at www.nfhs.com

ORDERING INFORMATION

PURCHASE ORDERS are welcomed but all orders under $50 must be prepaid. Purchase orders may be **either faxed or mailed** to our Customer Service office. If you mail a purchase order after it has been faxed to our Customer Service office, please show it as a **confirming order**. All back-ordered items will be billed additional shipping charges. Terms net 30 days per invoice. All delinquent accounts are charged 1.5% finance charges. **PREPAID ORDERS** will be shipped upon receipt of completed order form accompanied by a check or money order. **All orders must include the proper amount for shipping and handling.**
*SHIPMENTS OUTSIDE UNITED STATES OR CANADA: Please write to NFHS headquarters for a quotation of total charges which will include a $2.00 surcharge and actual shipping charges. **Payment must be in U.S. dollars.** Please refer to www.nfhs.com to view our Return Policy.